even the olives are bleeding
the life and times of Charles Donnelly

Photograph from "Connolly Column", 1979 New Books, Dublin

Charles Donnelly
1914 – 1937

even the olives are bleeding

the life and times of charles donnelly

joseph o'connor

NEW
ISLAND
BOOKS

Dublin

**even the olives are bleeding
the life and times of charles donnelly**
is first published by
New Island Books
2 Brookside,
Dundrum Road,
Dublin 14.

ISBN 1 874597 15 4

A catalogue record for this book is available from
the British Library.

New Island Books receives financial support from
The Arts Council (An Chomhairle Ealaíon), Dublin,
Ireland.

Cover Design by Jon Berkeley.
Typesetting by Rapid Productions.
Printed in Ireland by Colour Books Ltd., Baldolye.

CONTENTS

ACKNOWLEDGEMENTS

This book is substantially based on my MA thesis, *The Life and Work of Charles Donnelly*, (University College Dublin, 1986). My supervisor was Professor Seamus Deane, for whose thoughtful criticisms, insights and suggestions I am very grateful. The thesis may be examined by writing to the Head Librarian at UCD.

I would like to thank a number of other people for their help. These are: Professor Augustine Martin, Doctor Michael Paul Gallagher, the late George Gilmore, Michael O'Riordan, Colm Tóibín, Catríona Crowe, Joseph and Kay Donnelly, Cherry Murphy.

I would like to thank the staff of University College Dublin Library, the National Library of Ireland and the Marx Memorial and British Museum Libraries in London.

Special thanks are due to Marie O'Riordan, to my father, Sean O'Connor, and to Dermot Bolger, for publishing this book.

INTRODUCTION

Charles Donnelly is a ghost who haunts the pages of Irish literature. His elusive presence is everywhere; in poems by Donagh MacDonagh and Ewart Milne, in essays, in newsaper articles and in memoirs, in popular songs, in histories of the Irish Left and in the footnotes of academic theses. Everyone knows a little about Charles Donnelly and nobody knows very much.

His poems have never been widely published. Scholars have not had easy access to his papers, and the only biography to have appeared is a short and idiosyncratic work written by a member of his family, and therefore almost of necessity unobjective. His short stories, journalism and military historical writings have not been published by the family and are now almost completely forgotten. This man who wrote thousands of words is famous for only five spoken ones. His dying words. *Even the olives are bleeding.*

But there are a lot of questions still to be asked about Charles Donnelly and about the constructed nexus of distortions and silences which has enfolded him since his death in the olive groves of Spain almost fifty five years ago. This book is an attempt to answer some of those questions. It is time for the truth now. It is time for the silence to end.

Charles Donnelly always had a fear of being made a martyr. Yet this is precisely what has happened to him. In death he has been signed up and recruited much more thoroughly than he ever was in his activist life. To the political Left, he is one of the glorious fallen, a hero who laid down his life for the dictatorship of the proletariat. To others, he is a good Catholic boy turned against his father and his class by irreligious and irresponsible subversives. A number of people have taken Charles Donnelly and reinvented him. And a number of people have remained silent about the uncomfortable facts of his short life and violent death.

All stories are stories about children and parents. Charles Donnelly's story is no exception. The mercurial personality of his father looms over everything that he did. Some would say that rebelling against his father was the cornerstone of Donnelly's life, yet this, too, would be a distortion. His father was not a monster. He was a decent man, in fact, whose life did not work out the way he had planned it. But he despised the values that his son came to espouse, as deeply as his son despised his own. He believed in the kingdom of God in heaven; his son believed that human society could be perfected. Perhaps both beliefs are equally valid; perhaps they are both equally absurd. But the struggle between these two men is one of the central conflicts in Charles Donnelly's life.

In the fifty five years since his death very little of substance has been written about Charles Donnelly. What has been published is frequently too short, clichéd or inaccurate. The same sketchy biographical details, tortuous justifications and political mis-conceptions have at times been repeated to the point of predictability.

This book attempts to describe the facts of his life as fully as possible, based on his own writings, on interviews with his brother, his friends and political associates, and on written accounts of him by students, writers and political activists, many of whom are now dead. His childhood and adolescence, his school days and university career are discussed, as well as his family relationships, his love affair with Cora Hughes and the factors which led him to creative expression, political commitment and early death. His literary and ideological influences are outlined here. And the sometimes complex relationship between his politics and his poems is analysed.

This book, in short, is an attempt to provide a detailed and comprehensive introduction to Charles Donnelly's life, poetry and politics. He deserves that much, surely. It is important that more should be known about this shy and courageous man. He was a talented poet and an intelligently compassionate politician. Had he lived he might have become a major figure in Irish history. But speculation like this is a waste of time, and, in any case, when Samuel Beckett wishes the curse of an honourable name on his enemies he has a point. Charles Donnelly was a very private individual who lived in an ideologically demanding public world. It was a world where the only real revolutionary act was to think independently. He was never a slave – to his family, to his art, or to the political causes in which he believed. He makes a very poor icon. His ruthless individualism led him to despise what he called "the masked servilities" of convention. Ultimately, this increases the meaning of his actions and his poems.

The purpose of art is nothing less than to contribute to human freedom. But very few poets die for human freedom as well. It may appear naïve and stupid to be so idealistic, but Charles Donnelly was neither of these. He wrote, lived and died because of his profoundly intelligent commitment to the possibility of a better world. We don't have to share his commitment to understand it. But if we deny it, we deny everything about him.

11

For those who are completely lacking in idealism themselves it is convenient to be dismissive of people like Charles Donnelly. And for those whose idealisms would be inimical to his, it has been very easy to keep silent. But the uncomfortable facts of his life are still there. For a long time they have been forgotten about.

This book is an attempt to remember.

CHAPTER ONE

If you drove a few short miles out of Dungannon, in County Tyrone, in the troubled and weary province of Ulster, you would find yourself surrounded by lush green farmland. It would be very quiet here. You might see the occasional British army unit on patrol. You might see tourists, or people from south of the border buying cheap petrol. You might wonder about what could be going on in this landscape, what it might hide in itself. And you might wonder how such a silently beautiful place as Killybrackey could still exist in a part of the world where violent death barely makes the television news anymore.

Nearly eighty years ago, an extraordinary man was born here. Charles Patrick Donnelly was his name.

He was born on 10 July, 1914, at Killybrackey House, in the townland of Killybrackey, just outside Dungannon in County Tyrone. The house was bright, airy, comfortable, a family home, and a symbol in troubled times of the hard-won prosperity of that family. Houses are symbols in Ireland. Houses are ways of telling the world about yourself.

Killybrackey had been the Donnelly family home since the 1860's when it had been built by Charles Donnelly, the poet's grandfather, in the middle of thirty acres of the best farmland in the county. When Charles's son Joseph married a local girl, Rose McCaughey, in 1912, he took over the house, the land and the family business. He was a man whose time had come.

For generations, the Donnelly family had been

13

cattle breeders. They were tough, pragmatic, efficient. They were uninterested in politics, or in life beyond the hedges and ditches of their well-tended fields. The men were gruff and laconic. The women believed in hard work and frugal living. Their priorities were almost purely economic and apolitical, in that peculiarly Irish sense wherein conservatism disguises itself as being anti-ideological. The Donnelly's were well-respected. They had no time for the petty sectarianisms of rural Irish life. They mixed well with their Protestant neighbours. They mixed with anyone with whom they could do business. These people were friendly and tolerant. But above all else they were tough. They were survivors. The wider world would change, but their place in it would not. "They weren't looking for a Parnell or anyone else to lift them," Joe Donnelly, the poet's brother once said, "they would lift themselves."

This was the world that Charles Donnelly was born into. It was a world from whose values of independent thinking and cool assessment he would learn a great deal. But it was also a world which contained within itself the seeds of the contradictions which would lead him to question its entire foundation, and, ultimately, to reject it.

As a young boy Charles Donnelly was lively, mischievous and bright. His family recall many stories of childhood pranks, practical jokes, long summer days spent wandering the idyllic countryside around Killybrackey. He attended the local school where he got on well with the other children and made good progress. People liked him. He was, by all accounts, a happy child, with a playful affection for his parents, his brothers and sisters, and his extended family of aunts, uncles and cousins.

Things went well for the Donnelly family during the

14

early years of Charles Donnelly's life. His parents were fond of each other. They were good companions, and their marriage was happy. Whenever his father could, he bought more land and extended his farm. The business was improving all the time. And yet Joseph Donnelly was becoming gradually disenchanted with the limitations of his life.

He began slowly to look beyond the little townland for a future. And as time passed, he decided that he wanted to move away from the land, move to a country town, maybe open a shop there.

He felt unable to do this while his father was alive. The Donnelly family had lived on the land for generations, after all. They were just not town people. But when the old man died in 1917, Joseph Donnelly made his decision. He sold the farm, the house, the land, everything his father had worked for. He and his wife and his young family moved to Dundalk, where he opened a greengrocer's shop in Church Street. Joseph Donnelly began the resolute journey to move his family from one social class to another.

Joseph and Rose Donnelly worked hard. Their business thrived, and using the profits, Joseph bought some land outside the town in order to continue his cattle dealing. Every acre he bought and every pound in the bank insulated his family even more from the world. He made plans for his wife and his children. They would have the things that a prosperous man's family should have. He began to buy up dilapidated houses, renovate them and rent them out. Joseph Donnelly became a landlord. He became a man who believed in property, and in making money work. He became a man who believed in the capitalist system that his eldest son would one day come to despise.

But these were years of happiness for the young

couple. They enjoyed the benefits of town life, and yet were still close enough to Tyrone to visit regularly. As they became more prosperous, they had more children. Charles began to attend the local Christian Brothers school where he was a keen and open student. But even at this early age the future poet was developing the sceptical frame of mind that would have such serious consequences for the family in the years to come. His family recall Charles's father bringing him to the cattle market on one occasion. The child watched his father buy some cattle early in the day, which he sold at a profit a few hours later. The seven-year-old Charles was intrigued and insistent. How could the animals be worth more in one corner of the market square than another, he wanted to know. Joseph Donnelly was taken aback. He attempted to explain the rudiments of market economics to his son, with little success. Later on, he was so concerned by Charles's question that he consulted a priest about the matter. It was to be the first of many such concerns.

Gradually the family became more involved in the local community, as respected in the town as they had once been in the country. The Donnelly's were a decent family, people thought. They were the kind of people you could rely on. And even the War of Independence, which by 1920 was threatening to engulf the whole country, did little to dislodge the secure foundations of their insular world.

The struggle ended with the signing of the Anglo-Irish treaty by that section of the nationalist movement which Charles Donnelly was later to attack so vigorously in his polemical writing. In the bloody Civil War that followed, Donnelly's father was a supporter of the pro-treaty faction, Griffith and Collins and, later, WT Cosgrave. Joseph Donnelly did not like extremists. He was suspicious of hardline

16

Republicanism. At mass on Sundays he listened to priests denounce the rebels. They were Communists, he was told. They were subversives and criminals and they were not to be trusted. Joseph Donnelly believed all of this. He was just not the kind of man to ask questions.

In case there was any doubt, the bishops issued regular diktats from their palaces, instructing the faithful:

No-one is justified in rebelling against the legitimate government ... The opposite doctrine is false, contrary to Christian morals and opposed to the constant teaching of the Church .... Such being the Divine Law, the guerrilla warfare now being carried on by the irregulars is without moral sanction ... All those who, in contravention of this teaching, participate in such crimes, are guilty of the gravest sins, and may not be absolved in Confession, nor admitted to Holy Communion. In all this there is no question of mere politics, but of what is morally right or wrong ... We desire to impress on the people the duty of supporting the National Government, whatever it is; to set their faces resolutely against disorder; to pay their taxes, rents and annuities; and to assist the government, in every possible way, to restore order.[1]

Ten years later the same bishops were actively to support rebellion against the legitimate and elected government of Spain. But back in the twenties, the hypocrisies of the Irish Catholic church simply went unnoticed. Like most middle-class Catholics, Joseph Donnelly was resolute in his opposition to the Republicans. They were dangerous, he thought, and if they got the chance they would take away everything he had. Every evening when work was over, he led a rosary in his home to invoke divine

17

help in the destruction of Eamon de Valera and his Bolshevik henchmen.

But even during this most savage of conflicts, Joseph Donnelly's principal concerns were his family and his business interests. By 1925 he and Rose had had seven children: six boys and a girl. The couple decided that they needed a new home to accommodate comfortably their large and growing family. They planned to move from the centre of the town and out into the green suburbs that evoked the memory of their rural past. Work began on building the new home in 1926, and was completed by February 1927, just after the birth of Charles's sister, Carmel. Joseph and Rose were delighted with the spacious new house. But these were to be the last days of optimism and hope.

Shortly after giving birth, Rose Donnelly caught a virus which led, very quickly, to a streptococcal throat. She became very ill, and nothing could be done to save her. Within a week this beautiful and generous woman was dead. Joseph Donnelly was inconsolable. His aspirations died with her. Her death on 27 February 1927, ten years to the day before the death of her eldest son in Spain, heralded many changes for the Donnelly family and marked the end of Charles's childhood with a bitter finality.

He was thirteen years old.

But Joseph Donnelly had little time to mourn. Immediately after his wife's death, he and his eight young children moved to their new home, "Moorlands". The new freedom of the open countryside was a source of delight and adventure to the children, but for Joseph Donnelly this was a terrible time. He had lost not just a wife, but also a helpmate and partner, and he quite simply did not know how to cope. He was forced to rely on his son Charles for help with the younger children. He was forced to neglect his business interests. The world he had built over so many years began overnight to fall apart, and the pressure that put on him was almost unbearable. His children recall seeing their father sitting in silence at the kitchen table in the family home, head in hands, depressed, anxious and fearful for his children's future and his own. It must have been a painful sight.

Joseph had two sisters who lived in Dublin. They owned rented property in the city, and had lived there for many years. But to help with the children, Minnie and Lizzie Donnelly began to take it in turns to visit Dundalk, staying for weeks at a time. They wanted to help their brother. Yet in several important ways their presence only made things worse.

The two old unmarried ladies were strict Catholics and unrelenting disciplinarians, more interested in saving the souls of these six and seven year old sinners than in providing them with the love and support their mother's death had so suddenly removed. Hell, to these women, was as real a place as Dublin. They believed in saying prayers. They believed in punishment. Life for the Donnelly children was to become very hard.

It was around this time in the mid 1920's that Charles Donnelly began to take an interest in reading and in writing. The details of how this came about are vague. His brother says, that all he remembers is that when Charles started writing he was always writing. He was contributing to *Our Boys* even in Dundalk. and there was a controversy about a story he wrote about the Civil War which was rejected by the editor of *Our Boys*, who was an Englishman. Years later, in a BBC interview, Joe Donnelly recalled trying to locate it thirty years afterwards and how the librarian could still remember the incident.[2]

But if young Charles Donnelly began his interest in literature and politics in these years, it was strongly discouraged by his two aunts. With the true joylessness of the religious enthusiast, books were seen as morally suspect, sources of foreign ideas and sexual depravity. The ladies would not allow books into the house unless they were lives of the saints, or Catholic Truth Society pamphlets. Books, they thought, were a dangerous waste of time. There were more important things to worry about than books. And so in the name of piety, the bright young boy with the enquiring mind was forced to smuggle reading material into his own home.

Still, he began to read regularly, and he continued his experiments with writing also. His contributions to *Our Boys*, the Christian Brothers' magazine, display the exuberance and enthusiasm in the discovery of words that is always there in the early work of a young writer. Charles Donnelly began to reinvent the world. Considering that his home life was now so utterly wretched, this is hardly surprising.

From his youthful tales of handsome detectives, master spies and cunning criminals we may speculate that the crime novels of Agatha Christie or Chesterton may have been among those smuggled into the Donnelly home. Here in the pages of *Our Boys*, between articles on boy saints, national heroes and hurley sticks, young Charles Donnelly wrote stories about "The Case of the Rifled Safe", with opening lines like

Detective Inspector George Caulfield of Scotland Yard leant back contentedly in the graceful sheraton chair and pulled luxuriously at his Havana.[3]

Subversive stuff, indeed. No wonder his old aunts were worried.

The two pious ladies always remained unconvinced about their nephew's reading and writing, and they never gave up their attempts to stop it. There were furious arguments, but the young teenager fought stubbornly back. They turned to his father for help, but they found little. Joseph Donnelly was not interested in books himself, but at first he could see no reason to discourage the boy. His own father had been a well-read, self-educated man, and he felt that his sisters were being too zealous. His son was a little wild, he admitted, a little high-spirited and opinionated, but this was only natural in a boy of that age. The ladies gave him an ultimatum. They were tired of looking after Charles and his brothers and sisters, with no assistance from him, and they were tired of the constant travelling to and from Dublin. He would have to move his family to the capital, they insisted. Educational opportunites were better there, and they would be able to maintain their vigilance over the children's sinful souls while not neglecting their own business interests.

So in 1928, when Charles Donnelly was fourteen years old, his family moved to Dublin, where his father had bought a large house in Mountjoy Square. Charles began to attend the O'Connell School at North Frederick Street, in the heart of Dublin's inner city. But it was not a happy period in the young boy's life. The rebellious spirit he had shown in Dundalk became increasingly pronounced, and following a series of confrontations at school he was expelled after only a few weeks. It is perhaps a sign of priorities in the Donnelly family that his father did not even find out about this for many months.

Unhappy, restless and bored, young Charles Donnelly spent his days wandering the streets of the strange and fascinating city. His surviving jottings from this time reveal a desperately lonely adolescent, crying out for the love and acceptance which he was being so vigorously denied.

Words became a consolation. He read Joyce's *Dubliners* and he continued to write himself. He struggled with words, trying to force them into meaningful shape. He worked hard to mould his new-found literary perceptions into clarity. But things were about to change for Charles Donnelly. During that miserable first year in Dublin, new perceptions began to take hold of his questioning young mind.

The area of the city in which the prosperous Donnelly's lived was bordered at that time, as it still is today, by some of the most impoverished areas in Europe. Here in the filthy slum dwellings and crumbling tenements around North Richmond Street and Gardiner Street was hopelessness. Here was where people lived and died in squalor. Here was poverty on a scale he could never have seen before, all within half a mile of his comfortable, middle-class home. This had a powerful emotional effect on Charles Donnelly.

He began to go to the slums. He befriended families who lived there, and was appalled by what he saw of their lives. Many years after this time, an aunt was to remember meeting him one day as he was returning home from the tenement streets. He had tears in his eyes, she recalled, and he was very shocked. He had just visited a poor family. There were rats, he told her, in the tiny room where the children had been sleeping. There were rats running around in the room. He could not understand it. He simply could not believe that people could be forced to live like this. Returning home to his landlord father that afternoon, Charles Donnelly must have asked himself some searching questions.

The only political groups who cared about the

stinking morass into which the new Ireland had consigned its working people were the militant Republican IRA and Saor Eire. In the vile slums of Dublin, Donnelly met their activists. He began to associate with these women and men, to listen to their words and to read their publications. They told him the fundamental truth, that the poor were not poor because of inadequacy, or laziness, or bad luck. These people were poor, they told him, because other people were rich.

The response of the church to these groups was frenetic. The pastoral letter of 1931 is indicative of hierarchical concern:

We cannot remain silent in face of the growing evidence of a campaign of Revolution and Communism, which, if allowed to run its course unchecked, must end in the ruin of Ireland, both soul and body ... A new organisation entitled "Saor Eire" is frankly communistic in its aims. Its published programme is to impose upon the Catholic soil of Ireland the same materialistic regime, with its fanatical hatred of God, as now dominates Russia and threatens to dominate Spain. Materialistic Communism, in its principles and actions, wherever it appears, means a blasphemous denial of God and the overthrow of Christian civilisation. It also means class warfare, the abolition of private property, and the utter destruction of family life ... Surely the ranks of Communism are no place for an Irish boy of Catholic instincts. You cannot be a Catholic and a Communist. One stands for Christ, the other for Anti-Christ.[4]

The government's attitude was equally hysterical. In independent Ireland, the land of rebels and revolutionaries, dissent was now a criminal offence. Saor Eire, the IRA and Peadar O'Donnell's

Revolutionary Workers' Groups were proscribed. People who wanted to feed the poor were thrown into jail. The fascist-admiring General Eoin O'Duffy, Chief Commissioner of the Garda Síochana, spent his time amassing files on Communist tyrants who were about to take over the country. Ireland, in the years when Charles Donnelly came to political awareness, was an atrophying, priest-ridden society that had abandoned its egalitarian ideal in favour of a forlorn confessional state.

In understanding Charles Donnelly, it is important to remember all of this. We cannot forget that Donnelly's father was a man of property. He was a fervent supporter of the bishops and the Cosgrave government. He took his political and moral leadership from these men. His son, on the other hand, was beginning by his mid-teens to align himself with the radical movement, with the anti-establishment, with everything that his father despised. The observation that a young boy had made on a fair day in Dundalk had been sharpened and matured by what he had seen in the slums. Charles Donnelly began to question the religious and political structures into which he had been born. He began to reject the place in the new middle-class which his father had worked so hard to make his legacy.

As the months passed and his nascent political beliefs became more focussed, the lines were drawn in the Donnelly family. In the furious arguments that followed between Charles and his aunts, they made their position clear. His soul was in mortal danger, they argued. To deny the authority of the bishops and the government was in effect to deny God, and the orderly structures that God had intended for human life: unless Charles was prepared to find his place within those structures he would be in very

24

serious trouble indeed. They insisted that he see a priest, in the hope that a little theological patter would help him see the error of his ways. The priest outlined the evils of Communism. Charles Donnelly argued back, admonishing the reverend father, enthusiastically quoting Christ's injunction to give away one coat if you had two.

His aunts continued to plead and threaten. But all of this made Charles Donnelly even more determined not to be constrained by religious hypocrisy and empty notions of respectability. He continued to rebel, and yet this was to prove much more than teenage rebellion. He began to call himself a Republican and a Socialist. The ladies must often have looked back longingly on the days when their nephew's reading material had been the only family problem.

When persuasion failed, they came up with another solution. What their nephew needed, they decided, was a spell of good hard work. This would cure him of idle speculation on the plight of the poor. With the agreement of his father, they arranged for Charles to take an apprenticeship with one of their tenants, a carpenter. Charles did not argue. He took the apprenticeship, but refused to stop his self-education. He worked in the shop during the day. At night, he read Larkin's speeches and the writings of James Connolly. He attended lectures at the Workers' College in Dublin's Eccles Street. He associated openly with Communists. He refused, in short, to do what he was told.

The two ladies came up with one last strategy. They turned on their brother. This was all his fault, they maintained. He was obviously incapable of exerting a steadying influence on his children without a wife by his side. They began to urge him to re-marry. Joseph Donnelly refused. As a staunch traditionalist he believed that marriage was a life-long commitment, and that to marry again would be to insult the memory of his first wife. They insisted and he refused again, and still Lizzie and Minnie Donnelly would not be defeated. They had a sister who was a Holy Faith nun. They warned Joseph Donnelly. If he would not do what they suggested, they would arrange for her to leave her convent and come to look after the children. This was finally too much for him to countenance. Very reluctantly, Joseph Donnelly backed down, feeling he had no choice.

Joseph Donnelly proposed to one of his tenants, a dress designer, Maria Farrelly. They were married in October, 1930.

Perhaps not surprisingly, the marriage was not a happy one.

CHAPTER TWO

Joseph Donnelly's second marriage was to have a profound effect on his family. Charles Donnelly's new stepmother was an intelligent and warm-hearted woman, sophisticated, worldly-wise, sceptical. She was less concerned to save the children's souls than to give them a loving and stable home life. She was very calm and she was very tough, prepared to respect the two old aunts, but not to listen to their advice. Their influence would no longer be felt, she decided, in what was now her home. She made other decisions also. She told her husband that Charles was wasting his time learning a trade, and that a young person of his intelligence should be given the opportunity of a university education.

Donnelly's father agreed, reluctantly. So Charles left his apprenticeship in the carpenter's shop, and he began the three month intensive study course which would lead to his matriculation to University College, Dublin.

Donnelly entered UCD in October 1931 and he enrolled to take an Arts degree. His chosen subjects were Logic, English, History and Irish but he was to spend little enough of his time at UCD in the lecture hall or the library.

During the early thirties the college was a lively community in the centre of Dublin with elegant buildings at Newman House and Earlsfort Terrace. UCD had a good name, and, importantly, in those years, a sense of its own arrival. The War of Independence and Civil War were over, and education would play a vital role in the peace. Here was Cardinal Newman's dream made flesh and stone, a Catholic Irish University for an independent Irish state. Here were the children of the revolution. The young men and women who held the future in their hands.

From his home where books were seen as suspect, Charles Donnelly suddenly found himself in a milieu of intellectual debate, political argument, amateur philosophising on a grand and noisy scale. It must have seemed an extraordinary liberation. For the first time in his life Charles Donnelly was surrounded by people of his own age, many of whom shared his literary interests. He wasted no time. It was during his first month at UCD that he published his first poem, the Keatsian lyric, "Da Mihi":

Give me thy redness, love-sighing Rose,
Thy blushing tenderness be my heart!
That I may feel,
May, love-taught, feel
My fellow creatures' woe;
That my song may be kind,
My verse warm, lined
With truth such as angels know;

His mind was already turning to the humanising role of poetry in a heartless and impoverished world. But Donnelly was not the only wide-eyed young writer at UCD. In fact, there was a remarkable collection of literary talent at the college during these years. The poets Denis Devlin, Brian Coffey, Mervyn Wall and Niall Montgomery were all young students and became his friends. Donnelly met Brian O'Nuallain, who had not yet become Flann O'Brien, but who was nevertheless already creating his invented personas and fabulous literary concoctions.

He befriended the short story writer, Mary Lavin, and the future President of Ireland, Cearbhall O'Dalaigh. He knew the actors Liam Redmond and Cyril Cusack. He was closest to Donagh MacDonagh, son of the executed 1916 leader, and to Niall Sheridan, his flatmate and fellow poet.

Sheridan was editing the student magazine, *Cothrom Féinne*, during Charles Donnelly's first year. Decades later, he recalled his initial meeting with the young writer:

> *A typescript came in from someone I had never heard of, called, I think, Death Song, and written in a rather high-flown style, reminiscent of the Fenian cycle. It was nothing extraordinary, but there was some quality in it that I thought was interesting, and so I wrote to him and asked him to come and see me.*[5]

This first encounter was to be something of an anti-climax:

> *I arranged to meet him in the Main Hall of the college, then the only available rendezvous for students ... I had somehow got the idea that Donnelly would be a tall, fair-haired and athletic medical student. It was a bad guess. He turned out to be of less than average height, diffident in manner, with a lean earnest face and blue eyes of extraordinary clarity. He looked absurdly young.*[6]

The two young men liked each other immediately. This meeting was to be of importance to Charles Donnelly, as it was to lead him gradually into a group of close friends and to give him a forum in which to publish his work. He began to contribute regularly to *Cothrom Féinne*, writing essays on politics, literary criticism, modern philosophy.

29

During his first year he experimented with styles and subjects, trying to clarify his artistic interests, not always very successfully.

His piece, "Philistia: An Essay in Allegory", has all the passion and clumsiness of the undergraduate radical:

Eyeless, indeed, they are; stricken blind, worshipping in their temple which is Darkness, but which they call, and believe to be, Light ... Many and bestial idols do they worship in that gloomy temple of sighs: the dark tyrant god, Convention, who is the symbol of the clouds of Darkness, and the puffing winds of Weakness, which would be Strength ... the dark goddess, Ignorance, who is a monster of iniquity, and swallows the deformed lead-eyed children she begets.[7]

And the piece which prompted the invitation to meet Sheridan – "The Death Song" – seems almost laughably pretentious:

The red lipped morning kissed a smile to the face of the mountain land ... On the grassless brink of a grim fissure, tall Conal, the poet, stood, a dark and sinister figure, bent forward tensely, his cloak flowing behind him, his hair wild with the wind, his face as dark as the sky ... And when they whispered to each other that Conal was mad, his soul laughed within him and he did not speak. But when he sang his magic piercing songs, men's souls trembled in their eyes and when breath came to them they swore that the women were right, and that the poet was a god.[8]

It is amusing to see Donnelly pushing the standard wish-fulfillment myth of the young writer, that poets are somehow more sexually attractive than other unfortunate people. It must have been a very good

30

line to try out at the university bar. But buried in the middle of this slightly trying stuff was another Charles Donnelly poem. Nothing wonderful, perhaps. But yet, even in this lush Romantic lyric, the seventeen-year-old poet seems already capable of linguistic virtuosity and insight:

This life is but a walking sleep
Above a dark unwanted Deep,
Then, waken soul, and wildly leap,
And life is won!

Burst forth my song to Eternity,
And thunder like the cave lunged sea,
And I, my song, will follow thee,
Will follow thee!

As time passed, he broadened his horizons. In addition to his experiments with verse, Charles Donnelly began to write prose fiction at UCD. His short story, "People", is quirky and effective:

The other old man is smoking too. He is a ponderous old man, and dull and heavy, and pale and moisty, like a bag of damp flour: he is not as the first old man, who is small and brown, and like a foggy day ... The man who is nearly old is not smoking, because he neither smokes nor drinks. He is very hateful.[9]

And he continued to write journalism also, rapidly finding a wry, sensitively intelligent voice in which to express some of the new perceptions which were exciting him. These pieces are alive with energy, with the young writer's joyous discovery of the intellectual world.

In this article, for instance, Donnelly answers a stuffily pious student hack who had critised Yeats for being both un-Christian and unintelligent. The young poet was already learning to take up his corner and fight:

The implication is, of course, that Christianity and intelligence are essential qualities of a great artist. For an artist to be really great – I have always looked on the author of The Countess Cathleen *as being a really great artist, but that is a matter of personal opinion – his orthodoxy must be beyond question, and he must be as intelligent as, I presume, our friend, the man in the street. Christianity is, then, an essential quality in an artist. Well, to keep to the Moderns, Rousseau is not an artist. Nor Shelley. The* Prometheus Unbound *is not art. Byron's noblest passages are not even third-rate literature. Swinburne, Rossetti, Hardy, Ibsen, of course, have no claim to greatness. And the model of our young poets is to be Mrs Hemans, and the goody goody books of the nineties, and the inane matter entitled* Religious Poetry *in our modern weeklies. It would be singularly disappointing for Mr Yeats, above all poets, to hear this view expressed by a thoughtful and clever young writer of the new generation; Mr Yeats, above all persons, who battled so long against the penny-a-line Christianity of the Irish Grub-Street, and the bigotry and intolerance of zealotism.*

Art is free; and where there is no freedom there can be no Art, because in its freedom lies its value and its essence. If you trammel art, though with fetters of gold, you kill it; you take away its vitality, its soul. There may be people who would prefer a Mr Yeats who would express in conventional verse their conventional ideas. These "Christians" are no more capable of appreciating the poetry of William Butler Yeats than they are capable of understanding the philosophy of Christ. It was the outraged spirit of this

32

conventionalism which drove Shelley from Oxford, and Byron from England; it was this spirit which shrieked on the appearance of the beautiful lyrics of Swinburne's first series of Poems and Ballads. *Now, the* Poems and Ballads *are about as un-Christian as anything could be. Yet does anyone who claims to the slightest literary taste or discernment dare deny that they are Art, and great Art?*[10]

This article ends with another Keatsian touch. An impassioned and, affecting defence of the role of the imagination in human life:

There is a higher intellectual faculty than Reason; an intellectual power whose dictates often contravene those of Reason; but a power which has much more influence on men's lives and action than has Reason; a power which is at the bottom of all Art, and on the summit; which is the creator and the creation of Art; which is Art, and is the soul of Art, and the flesh. That quality is Imagination, the faculty of Intellectual Emotion; and the child of Imagination is Wisdom; the child of Reason, the shadow of Wisdom.[11]

Thus, early in his career at UCD, Charles Donnelly began to see himself as a writer. But he also began to think about the demands of creativity, and about the difficulties of imaginative writing in an ideologically backward society. In the article, "Literature in Ireland", he is already pondering the role of the artist in the public world. Written with the urgency of a political pamphlet, his argument outlines some of the problems:

Literature is not in a flourishing condition in Ireland … The modern Irish artist cannot throw over modern thought. Neither can he afford to throw over Ireland.

In his consciousness, the two must fuse. His problem is to accomplish that fusion. Modern Irish art must be in touch with the people. But the position is not so simple as it appears ... For to be of any importance it must be in touch with more than the people. The people must form the objective correlative of the emotions of Irish literature. But for production, that objective correlative must (in the mind of the writer) harmonize with his intellectual background. Not only has our artist to set his house in order, but he has to accommodate it to the landscape. And to reach his house at all, he has to cut his way through the clever and the facile and the semi-educated and political and literary charlatanry. The job isn't going to be an easy one. It will require a large amount of guts. But it's there to be done.[12]

Charles Donnelly was already thinking in large terms. University College Dublin provided him with the opportunity to write, to discover words and what he could do with their power. But it was also while he was at UCD that Donnelly began to find the intellectual structure that would shape his emotional response to the poverty he had seen in the Dublin slums. His literary interests were internationalist. This led him to an interest in contemporary philosophy, and to an application of philosophical thinking to politics. He began to read Bergson, William James, John Dewey, Whitehead, Bertrand Russell. And his work in *Cothrom Féinne* began to take a philosophical turn:

The modern mind is most obviously characterised by the complexity of its emotions, expression of which is no longer lyrical but palimpsestic. Interacting with this complexity is the concern for analysis of emotion, an analysis carried on with a wonderful integrity,

34

precision and subtlety. This keeness has brought about a recognition of the limitation of terms, a tautness of structure and a not always happy economy of sentiment.[13]

This article is called "The Trend of Modern Philosophy", and it is clear from the piece that Donnelly is opposed to the trend, which he sees exemplified in Bergson and Whitehead, to "solve the problem of the relation between appearance and reality by setting consciousness back in nature, by regarding perception as a relation between individuals". It is a clumsy article, jargonistic and dull. At one point Donnelly includes a long quote from Bergson to prove that he is not a materialist, which, as a letter writer to the magazine later pointed out, is a little like "quoting Lenin to prove he is a communist." Nevertheless, it is a vital source for tracing his political growth. By now, Charles Donnelly had begun to read more dangerous writers than Chesterton. He had begun to read Karl Marx.

Here, in the pages of the student magazine, is the very first occasion on which Charles Donnelly defended Communism, on philosophical grounds. He places the entire contemporary philosophical debate in political terms:

While actually human intellect is bedded in nature, while a great scarlet stain of human consciousness is slowly spreading into the very heart of the chaotic, unconscious, capitalist word, while intensifying consciousness is tautening art and literature and revolution, the professors, in their investigations of the traditional problems of knowledge are driven to a theoretical imbedding of consciousness in life ... In the person of Lenin, and in accordance with the principles of Marxism, mind has for the first time asserted its

35

rights as an element in nature, as an agent of fermentation. Lenin's attitude to opportunism in the Labour movement seems to me one of the most significant things in the history of thought. He formulated a theory accounting for the existence of a corrupt stratum of the working class: the theory of the function of "colonial super profits". Marx had already voiced this theory. But what Lenin stressed was its importance on the plane of action. Lenin has added a dimension to humanity.[14]

Thought and action. The two words which occur most often in Donnelly's poems, and in his other writings also. The young student was already anticipating the demands of activism. The demands which would ultimately lead him out of the lecture hall and into the world of the street.

University College Dublin underwent radical changes during Charles Donnelly's brief career there, and he was involved in many of them. When the Students' Union was established in 1930 it was controlled by students who were politically progressive and anti-fascist. But there were ultra-conservative elements in the college also, growing in strength all the time. Organisations like the Student Christian Movement and the Pro Fide Group – mocked in Donnelly's poem "The Dead" – were eventually to gain control of the Union in 1933. These were quite openly Fascist groups, sectarian, anti-semitic and right wing in their politics, often ruthless in their methods. They distributed fanatical anti-Communist and pro-Nazi propaganda, broke up meetings, intimidated left-wing students. As a committed young Communist, Charles Donnelly was an obvious target for their zeal.

In response to all of this, and also as a means of involvement in practical Leftist politics, Donnelly founded a small political group in UCD, calling it, somewhat dramatically, The Student Vanguard. Radical Republican leader Frank Ryan was invited to the inaugural meeting, which Donnelly's friend Donagh MacDonagh was asked to chair. MacDonagh, in his own words, "had never chaired anything" and was extremely nervous at the prospect, particularly when a large group of Blueshirt thugs arrived to break up the gathering. A minor riot ensued. MacDonagh recalled later:

The trouble started fairly soon and private fights of many kinds developed quickly all over the hall. I banged on the table but nobody took much notice, in fact the noise increased considerably. Then Donnelly jumped up on the table and shouted for order which he astonishingly got. After that, he took control of everything, including the chair. He put motions, passed resolutions and read the manifesto which he had written.[15]

A slightly bewildered MacDonagh goes on to recall one of the odder brief alliances in Irish political history:

He even managed to get the Blueshirts a safe conduct out of the building. They put up their knuckledusters and, under the protection of Frank Ryan, slipped down the stairs and away.[16]

His new-found political activity interfered with his studies, and Donnelly was frequently cautioned by his teachers. His literary interests created difficulties also. Independent to the point of stubbornness, he did not like his reading being organised. Indeed, one of his articles roundly satirises fellow students for only reading writers who were, in that greatest of undergraduate phrases, "on the course". He paid little attention to his lecturers, and, in fact, failed his first year examinations. He seems to have had very little time for the organized discipline of university study. He disliked academics and their way of life. "The chief critical discoveries of the past year in University College Dublin are not difficult to number", he wrote. "There is, first of all, the momentous discovery that King Lear contains sixty-seven references to nature, and the appropriate moral drawn from this and other facts in the play (a moral, if I may be permitted to quote the man in Chekhov's play, easy of comprehension and handy for home use.)"[17]

Despite his sceptical attitude to UCD's English Literature department, Donnelly continued to read privately, and to write poems. By the end of his first year his style had already begun to change. In poems like "Stasis", he began to lose the lush romanticism of the early verse and to move towards the logical taut voice which we associate with his mature work:

This is a sleeping place,
A cast shell
Of the snail of the world,
A thing left in a crevice.

He had by now developed wide-ranging literary interests. He admired the work of many of his student contemporaries, and, indeed, the sensitively intellectual voice of Denis Devlin in particular seems to have occasional echoes in Donnelly's poems. In addition, MacDonagh and Sheridan have recalled his deep knowledge of the work of Shelley, Blake, Charles Lamb, Eliot, the Elizabethan poets, Kafka, Rimbaud and Baudelaire. He loved the work of

Gerald Manley Hopkins (who had taught at UCD some years earlier). He loved Joyce and Yeats. Donnelly's undergraduate writings are littered with quotations from these writers, along with references to Huxley, Middleton Murray, Proust. And perhaps above all of these, he loved the work of John Keats, his passionate and elegant letters as well as his astonishing poems. Sheridan remembers:

He was attracted by the intellectual rather than the sensuous element in literature – a typical instance being his almost chronic preoccupation with Keats's phrase about "the earnest stars". It thrilled him in its manifestation of fine sensibility and unique complexity of thought.[18]

But Donnelly was no myopic bookworm. Literature, for him, did not exist on some higher and purer plane of existence. It came from the real world, and remained profoundly a part of that world. He scoffed at the invented categories of the English literature department. Indeed, he saw the whole notion of "English", as an academic subject, as ideologically suspect. Divisions broke down in his mind. Imaginative writers were already influencing his politics, and political thinkers were shaping his creative writing. Marx, for Donnelly, became the ultimate Romantic, and Keats the ultimate rebel. His favourite phrase from Keats, for example, turns up here, not in a piece on poetry, but in a concise essay on the rise of German Fascism:

Human development takes the form of a development in complexity of experience. When Keats saw "trees, branch-charmed by the earnest stars", his experience was more complex than that of the convent-school girl who sees "twinkling stars" or "golden stars" and than

*that of the man in the street who sees merely "stars".
It was more interfused with thought. A tension of the
spirit. You will have no difficulty in perceiving "a star",
"a twinkling star" or "a golden star" but it is only with
much effort and on a superb plane of consciousness
that you will reach a momentary perception of an
earnest star. I do not believe that Captain Goering is
ever likely to see an earnest star.*[19]

In addition to his exploration of the wider world
of books and writers, Donnelly spent his time at
UCD trying to persuade his new friends to his
political views. He often visited Sheridan and
MacDonagh at their boarding house in Rathmines,
always leaving behind, they later recalled, a
selection of Marxist literature. "He tried to convert
us" Sheridan remembers, "it was an absolutely
hopeless task."

But Donnelly was never purist in his politics. He
was deeply committed, but also tolerant and open-
minded. He liked intelligent people of most political
persuasions and of none. Though reticent and
thoughtful, he liked company. He liked parties.
MacDonagh recalls one of these drunken evenings
with remarkable clarity:

*I remember a party which we gave at our digs at
which many pints were lowered and many bad jokes
and puns were made, while Donnelly sat
with his back to the wall murmuring disgustedly
Keats's phrase, "What did I laugh tonight?" He and
a surrealist poet, now a diplomat, agreed that they
were the only important and serious people present,
which indeed they were. The rest were engaged in a
confused game of poker. Afterwards eight of our
guests climbed into a Baby Austin to go home,
Donnelly all the time reminding the driver to go*

*carefully. "You have a car load of geniuses aboard"
he said, "Irish literature depends on your brakes."*[20]

But the young poet was not always so relaxed as
MacDonagh remembers him here. There was another
side to Charles Donnelly. Those who knew him
constantly refer to his courage and generosity, his
knack of preserving friendships and his
understanding. Yet these qualities were balanced by
an intensity, a certain vulnerability and an almost
painful shyness. He was particularly uneasy about his
work, for example, and about the public perception of
it. WH Auden wrote that he could understand anyone
wanting to write poetry, but not wanting "to be a
poet." Donnelly would have understood what he
meant. He was very bad indeed at being a poet. In a
BBC radio documentary about his old friend, Niall
Sheridan recalled Donnelly's bashfulness:

*There was a considerable contrast between Don
[MacDonagh] and Charlie in the way they presented
their new works. If Don had a new poem in his pocket
he'd stop you in the street and hit you over the head
with it. He'd chain you to the railings until you heard
it all out. Charlie would very, very tentatively, almost
accidentally produce it, and one would have to work
on him to get him to read it.*[21]

Sheridan and MacDonagh felt that public
perception of their friend's insular personality was
not helped by his increasingly vehement political
beliefs. And I think we must accept this. Charles
Donnelly was a very serious young man. He was
certainly no student dilettante. He believed deeply in
the new politics he had found, and he was willing to
pay the cost. His commitment caused resentment
from some of his peers. They shared many of his

41

views, but not his ardour. Debating against the fascists in Newman House on a Saturday night was fantastically entertaining, but they simply wanted to enjoy being students. Charles Donnelly did not blame them. He just left them to it, and it probably suited him that way. He was discovering something important about himself: that he would never be happy being part of any group.

He became more of a loner. When he failed his examinations he had to repeat his first year, and Donnelly began to see less of his old classmates. This did not bother him in the slightest. His friends were now the IRA men and Communists he met at political meetings. His Marxist views and the intensity with which he pursued them had erected barriers between himself and his fellow students, but they were not important enough for him to break down. There were more important barriers to attack outside the cosy world of university life. Sheridan remembers how political activity inexorably started to take up most of his friend's time:

His interest in literature gradually began to take second place to his political interests. He was a convinced Marxist, and he believed in the perfectability of human society, an idea which seemed quite ludicrous to MacDonagh and myself. With that sort of belief went a slight lack of humour. He had irony, but he wasn't a humorous person, although he was a great audience for other people.[22]

Thus, by the end of his first year in college, the young poet was becoming increasingly drawn to the life of the political activist. Yet, interestingly, his poetry never reflects this. There are no poems about demonstrations or meetings or planned revolutions. For a Communist poet who began to write in the thirties, this is unusual, to say the least. The reasons why this should be so require brief explanation.

Charles Donnelly was by no means the only poet to commit himself to Communism during that decade. But different poets did this in different ways. There were, for instance, in Allen Tate's memorable words, "the well brought-up young men [who] discovered that people work in factories and mines, and wrote poems calling them Comrades from a distance."[23] Charles Donnelly was not one of these. But to find out what he was, we have to take a broad view.

The 1930's were years in which the demands of ideology were to become stronger all the time. During this decade, artists from all over the world committed themselves to political causes and movements more thoroughly than ever before. In Britain, for example, the decade following the carnage of World War One had thrown up new challenges to the notion of a pure and apolitical art operating in some ethereal dimension separate from everyday life. The poets of that war, especially Owen and Sassoon, were partially responsible for this. Their pity and raging passion spelt the end of the quaint notion of art for art's sake. An uneasy new sense of the social spread through the creative life of the country as writers and artists became ideologically polarised. Michael Roberts, who edited and published important work during the thirties, remembers the uncertainty out of which commitment would eventually emerge:

In that period, it seemed to us there was no finality. We learned to question every impulse until we became so self-conscious, so hag-ridden by doubts, indecisions, uncertainties, that we lost all spontaneity ... It was not any one thing which caused this scepticism: it appeared in various guises – the theory of relativity breaking up our neat mechanical world,

43

*science learning to doubt whether it could approach
any finality, psychoanalysis discovering how many
actions, apparently spontaneous, were rigidly
determined; and beyond all this a feeling: that the
middle class world, the world of the 19th century was
definitely breaking up, and that it would be replaced
in the near future by a world of Communism or big
business.*[24]

British writers were finding new, international
problems with which to engage. But Irish writers had
to contend with specifically national ones also. The
development of the post-revolutionary state had been
a bitter disappointment to most of them. Political strife
and disunity combined with widespread poverty, high
emigration and national xenophobia to produce a
warped culture. The new nation's political leaders
shared and propounded a highly selective version of
Irishness based on Catholic, rural and insular values.

It became increasingly clear in the years when
Charles Donnelly was starting to write that non-
conformism of any kind was to be punished. The
press became more conservative and determinedly
party political. The church preached adherence to a
particularly vicious form of Catholicism. Censorship
became widespread. The work of internationally
renowned authors was scanned by a new breed of
Irish thought police. Words like "freedom" and
"independence" littered the speeches of the nation's
leaders, while unemployment, hunger and a
hopelessly shortsighted economic policy forced tens
of thousands of the poor to seek refuge in the ghettos
of Boston and New York. Those who stayed were left
to eke out an existence in the slums of the cities, or
on the exhausted and barren farmland. Ireland's
leaders ruined Ireland, in the years when Charles
Donnelly was coming to maturity.

Throughout the 1920's and 1930's, Irish writers provided the most sustained, intelligent and vitriolic critique of the new regime. Yeats, Russell, Joyce and Gogarty pilloried governments throughout the twenties. In the thirties, the mantle was taken over by Liam O'Flaherty, Sean O'Faolain, Frank O'Connor and Peadar O'Donnell. In their sparse and bitter short stories they registered their anger at the selling out of the great Republican ideal.

That radical Republicanism ran through the literary tradition as far back as Wolfe Tone. And most important Irish writers since Tone had also been radicals. O'Casey, Shaw, Wilde, Synge and Joyce all described themselves as socialists, at one time or another. Of course, in a sense, this is an academic reconstruction. Joyce's socialism leaned far more towards anarchism; and Wilde's, with its emphasis on individual style, was equally vague and idiosyncratic. But the radical Irish literary tradition exists nonetheless.

Out on the edges of this tradition were the lonely voices that clearly and openly espoused the causes of the Left. There was Patrick McGill, the "navvy poet", whose *Songs From The Dead End* claimed for working class culture a humanist dignity robbed by colonial Irish society. There was Robert Tressell, whose *Ragged Trousered Philanthropists* became an essential socialist text. There was Jim Connell, the poet and Union organiser from Meath who composed the Left's great battle-hymn, "The Red Flag". As an Irish poet who was also a socialist Charles Donnelly is not some kind of historical freak. It is possible – and, I would argue, necessary – to read him as a strand of the Irish literary tradition which has always been politically radical.

But if Charles Donnelly's radicalism links him to some Irish writers, it separates him from them also.

45

His literary internationalism sets him apart from that group of progressive writers which would have included O'Faolain, O'Flaherty and Frank O'Connor. These had all fought in the independence struggle and had lived to see their work banned by the censors of the new Irish state. Their attacks on the hypocrisy and philistinism of that state were powerful and impressive. Stories like O'Connor's "Guests of the Nation" evinced an international influence yet were explicitly Irish in their concerns. The work of these three, and of Donnelly's UCD friend, Mary Lavin, presented versions of Ireland which were sharply at odds with Eamon de Valera's Celtic Disneyland.

But while these writers subverted the rhetoric of traditionalism, they simultaneously endorsed it also. They celebrated what Donnelly called "the juiciness of popular speech", the suffering and occasional triumph of the individual in the harsh world of Ireland. They hacked relentlessly at the facade of magical words built by the politicians and priests, and they exposed the grubby reality behind it. The short story writers were radical, but radically nationalist and reformist. There was another group which, by nature, was subversive and internationalist.

The most important of these were poets and Donnelly was to meet several of them at UCD. These were writers who were younger, and who had grown up in the post-revolutionary regime. Faced with the demands of living in a country whose values they were inimical to, many of them decided to look abroad for inspiration. Some left the country; others who stayed simply ignored it, at least in their writing. Most of them, except for Donnelly and one or two others, sold out in the end.

But in the early days, Denis Devlin, Mervyn Wall and Niall Montgomery experimented with surrealism and symbolism. Brian Coffey and Niall Sheridan read the work of Baudelaire and Rimbaud and were utterly uninterested in Irish literature. These were Donnelly's first real poetic influences. Although he read Irish writing, he had an absolute contempt for the "Celtic Twilight" writers whom, he argued, "had fitted irrelevant phrases to their cardiac conditions and called the result poetry."[25] He insisted on the importance for Irish poets of contemporary European thought, art and philosophy. His poems, with their urban settings and modernist experiments, their Freudian images and analogical concepts, are far more evocative of international writers than Irish ones.

In England, another group of young poets was simultaneously going in the same direction. This group – Stephen Spender, Cecil Day Lewis, Louis McNiece and, above all, WH Auden – became a major influence on Donnelly's writing. Like him they were university educated, middle-class, left wing and internationalist in outlook. They wrote poems about political events but they tried to keep the tone cool, intellectual, unemotional. Auden used bold new images from Marx and Freud, from science and from geography. Like Donnelly, he refused to write propaganda poetry for the Left, despite his personal views. "Poetry", he insisted, "is not about telling people what to do, but about extending our knowledge of good and evil ... only leading us to the point where it is possible to make a rational and moral choice." Charles Donnelly would certainly have agreed. His own poems – written during periods of immense political and personal upheaval – are always calm. They do not lecture.

They do not tell people what to do.

Time went on. One by one, Charles Donnelly's student friends took their places in the society they had once ridiculed. The bright young radical poets became diplomats, judges, politicians. Later one by one, the literary figureheads of the Left in the thirties would all abandon their pasts. Stephen Spender would say, that he had been talked into joining the Communist Party. Auden, speaking in the 1950s, would explain it all away:

Looking back, he said, it seems to me that the interest in Marx taken by myself and my friends ... was more psychological than political; we were interested in Marx the same way we were interested in Freud, as a technique in unmasking middle-class ideologies, not with the intention of repudiating our class, but with the hope of becoming better bourgeois.[26]

Charles Donnelly did repudiate his class, but he did not use his poetry to do it. Instead, he involved himself in class politics. He never saw his poetry as narrowly political. He never used his poems, either to become a better bourgeois, or a better Communist. He wrote his poems, and he fought for his beliefs. So, although Donnelly was influenced by Auden and the "Movement" poets, the difference between them does not just express itself as a difference of opinion about political activism.

It is a difference in understanding Marxism as a basis for poetry. It is a difference, in the end, in ways of looking at the world.

CHAPTER THREE

In 1932, WT Cosgrave's right wing government lost power to the Fianna Fáil party. Cosgrave's party had always been despised by the Left; it had spawned the fascist Blueshirts and repressed radical organisations with ferocity. The new Fianna Fáil government had tried to suppress the Blueshirt movement, but had also proscribed the IRA. To the Leftist veterans who were now Donnelly's associates, this was treachery. They saw Fianna Fáil, the self-styled "Republican Party", as a gang of craven opportunists who would betray the Republic and come to a political understanding with British Imperialism.

This was a massive problem for the IRA, and for progressives generally, because Fianna Fáil as a populist party continued to draw its strength from the small farmers, urban and rural workers who had always supported the independence struggle in the past. It was not that the Fianna Fáil leaders had abdicated their position at the forefront of that struggle. They had simply changed the nature of it and managed to keep their support.

Meanwhile, the IRA men who were now Donnelly's associates – George Gilmore, Frank Ryan and Michael Price – had decided on one last effort to push the movement into greater militancy, reclaiming the radical history they saw as running in a direct line through the Republican tradition from Wolfe Tone to Connolly. At the General Army Convention in 1934, Price proposed a motion redeclaring "our allegiance to the Republic of Ireland based upon production and distribution for use and not for profit."27

The motion was defeated. Price and his comrades left the IRA and started organising a nucleus of groups which was was to lead to the formation of "a congress of Republican opinion" to debate the struggle for Socialism in Ireland. Charles Donnelly joined this new Republican Congress.

Initially the group was quite successful. The Athlone Convention, which Donnelly attended, established a provisional working structure. The Congress began to attract broad working-class support on both sides of the border, and Congress activists started to involve themselves in local political issues. But before long, the founders and supporters of the group were to receive a severe setback. A group of Northern Protestant members was attacked by a gang of IRA men at the annual Wolfe Tone commemoration at Bodenstown cemetery. It was an ominous warning.

After this sectarian outburst, Donnelly was discouraged about the Congress's future, but he continued to work towards the first full meeting at the end of September. Through his work with the group, he was to find ways of making his politics meaningful. It was also through the Congress that he was to meet one of the most important people in his life.

Cora Hughes was a member of Cumann na mBann, and a close friend of Donagh MacDonagh and his sister, Barbara. Cora had an MA in Celtic Studies from UCD. She was independent, very intelligent, strikingly beautiful. She came from a staunchly nationalist family. Eamon de Valera was her godfather. Her father, a well-known Dublin doctor, was an old schoolfriend of the Republican leader, and had been best man at his wedding.

Like Donnelly, Cora Hughes was a rebel, against the capitalist system and against her family. She was a radical socialist who had joined the left-wing Republican Congress in open defiance of her parents' wishes. Her friend, Barbara Redmond [née MacDonagh] remembers the intensity of Cora's politics:

She was really a very Catholic person who had gone the other way, if you will. I find it hard to explain, but in her devotion to nationalism and socialism she was almost like a nun.[28]

Through their involvement in the Republican Congress, Cora and Donnelly began to spend time together. Very quickly, they became lovers.

Prior to her relationship with Donnelly, Cora had been involved with George Gilmore, a leading former member of the IRA and founder member of the Congress. Some fifty years after these events I met George in Dublin, and he could still remember the strength of the attraction between Donnelly and Cora. He showed me a very touching passage from his still unpublished novel, *The Gold Flag*. The section deals with the arrival of a younger man – a poet – into the heroine's life. The inspiration for these characters needed very little explanation. "It was the end of the romantic involvement between us", George told me. Despite that, he insisted, there was never any bitterness:

The three of us were always good friends and good comrades. With people like Charlie and Cora there would never be any question of small-mindedness or jealousy. I believe that Charlie loved Cora and that she returned that love. But it had a purity, almost a spiritual intensity to it, although it wasn't platonic,

51

*which meant that there was no room for meanness of
mind on anyone's part: least of all mine, because
Charlie Donnelly and I were closer than brothers.
Even though he was younger, he was old beyond his
years, politically and emotionally very mature. I loved
him almost as much as I love Cora – which is more
than a cynic like me would say is possible to love
anyone.*[29]

When news of Cora reached the Donnelly home, his
father was overjoyed. He knew that Charles had been
neglecting his studies, and that he had begun to
spend a good deal of his time on picket lines and
demonstrations around the city. He knew also that
his son had joined the newly formed Communist
Party of Ireland, and he was horrified. Joseph
Donnelly appears to have hoped that Cora would be
a stabilising influence on his son, but that goodwill
did not last very long. Charles's love affair with Cora
Hughes was rapidly to become another battle in the
war between father and son.

One day early in the relationship Cora called to the
Donnelly home. As his son was busy, Joseph
Donnelly took the opportunity to tell Cora how
delighted he was about her involvement with Charles.
He hoped, he told her, that everything would go well
for them, and that Charles would forget all about his
ludicrous politics. He hoped, that his son would get
some sense now. Cora was not so easily patronised.
During the ensuing argument she told Joseph
Donnelly in strong terms that she would certainly not
discourage Charles's activism, and that, in fact, she
would support it as much as she could.

From then on, Joseph Donnelly did everything he
could to end the relationship.

Cora's family never agreed with it. As traditional
nationalists and good Catholics they saw her interest

in Socialism as deeply dangerous, and her interest in Charles Donnelly as an element of that danger. The Hughes family and Joseph Donnelly tried as hard as they could to break the young couple up, but they found that they were unable to do so.

Charles and Cora continued their love affair, and their involvement with the leadership of the Republican Congress. But even in his political work Donnelly maintained his independence of mind and his elusive character. Always an outsider in a world of comradeship and common purpose, he believed, in the words of one of his poems, that as an activist "you give your services, but not yourself." Congress members from the time remember Charles Donnelly with respect and admiration, but with little affection. He could be bossy, they say, almost hostile. The more people agreed with his views, the less he seemed to like them. One Dublin activist, Paddy Byrne, recalled in a memoir that Donnelly "had shrewdness in some areas, and an almost fantastic naïveté in others."

What seemed like bossiness – even arrogance – was difficult for his comrades to take. But Charles Donnelly was developing the stubborn insistence on his own individuality which would inform his life and his poetry so utterly. And, of course, things went both ways. George Gilmore told me that the initial refusal of Congress members to accept fully this highly-strung middle-class poet into their ranks hurt the young idealist very deeply.

Nevertheless, throughout this period Charles Donnelly's relationship with Cora Hughes was a source of happiness and security to him. They were rarely apart. At social events, on marches or demonstrations they were always together. George Gilmore told me that Joseph Donnelly had been ironically correct in thinking that Cora would stabilize Charles Donnelly. "But stabilize him in his commitment to justice for the working people," he said, "and not his studies."

Part of the Congress campaign was a strong offensive on the problem of the Dublin slums. By now the Red Scare of the bishops was at its height. The people who lived in these hovels were being warned from gold-leafed pulpits not to listen to the Satanic inspired anarchists who were trying to organise them.

But since the beginning of the thirties the tenement problem had become too serious to be long held in check by their Lordship's pronouncements. Even the pro-government *Irish Times* was on the side of the tenants:

> *The Roman Catholic Hierarchy has warned its flock very urgently against the menace of Communism but the warning must be futile so long as 4,830 tenement houses shelter 25,320 families in the heart of Dublin. It is almost a miracle that hitherto Communism has not flourished aggressively in that hideous soil.*[30]

From the beginning of 1934, Congress groups stepped up their campaigns in these miserable areas. They posted parties of men to stop the poorest of families being evicted. They organised tenants into groups that ran rent strikes. They forced some of the worst landlords to repair their vile properties. Donnelly and Cora plunged into this work with tireless effort, campaigning, speaking on street corners, helping to organise enormous marches of thousands of the city's poor, under the Irish tricolour and the papal flag, to the Lord Mayor's residence on Dawson

Street and other symbolic centres of Irish power.

The establishment responded swiftly to challenges like this. Young Congress activists were frequently harassed and beaten by the police. Donnelly himself became a popular target. Groups of policemen would often congregate at the back of public meetings to arrest him.

He delighted in always escaping. But he would not escape for long.

Charles Donnelly's life was beginning to speed up now, as the demands of commitment became more pressing and more dangerous. He was harassed by the authorities. He was openly revolutionary. His relationship with his father was deteriorating all the time. And yet, in the middle of all this conflict, he continued to write precise, forcefully unemotional poems like "Approach", quietly debating the difficult role of the private individual in the public world:

> *The tightening eyes, tendrilled of sympathy,*
> *The accepted secret before a third;*
> *The unrequired gesture, imperfect denial of contact,*

These poems are thoughtful, measured, personal. But they are always aware of the world, also. Some explanation is required for this seeming paradox.

The question of private and public had been on the literary agenda in England for some time. (Auden's line "private faces in public places" had already been borrowed by Donnelly as the subtitle to one of his own poems), but the new found interest of the thirties poets in psychoanalysis had made it more self-consciously pointed. Many of these writers' attempts to deal with this question had been blunt and clumsy, as young poets vied with each other to display their ids and egos in the pages of the influential magazines *New Signatures* and *New Society*. But gradually it became clear to writers like Auden and Charles Donnelly that the question of the tension of public and private was not just a psychological one, but one that had political and aesthetic applications also.

In an incisive retrospective remark, Robin Skelton has written: "what gives the best of the period's poetry its unmistakable quality seems to be the way in which feelings of private and communal insecurity are fused together, so that the personal lyrical anguish informs the political statement."[31] Among the causes of this were the breakup of Victorian certainties and the carnage of the First World War. Eliot's *The Wasteland* (1922) was simultaneously the last great outcry of nostalgia for the past and the inauguration of a new historical context. Poetry could no longer be private. Younger poets began to place the traditionally private feelings of lyric poetry in the public world of history. Their poems became what Samuel Hynes has called "parables of immediate events upon private lives".[32]

A powerful poem by the Chilean Pablo Neruda outlines the conflict succinctly:

And you will ask: why does his poetry not
speak of dreams and leaves
and the great volcanoes of his native land?

Come and see the blood in the streets.
Come and see
the blood in the streets.
Come and see the blood
in the streets![33]

Private and public. The world of dreams, and the world of the streets. Most of Charles Donnelly's mature poems are concerned in some way with these conflicts. By 1934, his work has taken on a distinctive style. There is a new dramatic tension of opposite forces and ideas, usually with a detached and thoughtful tone. The poems become shorter, tighter, sharper, with tight and logically arranged structures sometimes borrowed from Auden. His English contemporaries give him access to their common fund of geographical and scientific symbolism. From Keats and Shelley he took precision and commitment.

There is a new emphasis on moral honesty in the writing, a new concern to analyse rather than apprehend an experience. And there is an attempt to rid his poetry of the "I", thus simultaneously adding to the dispassionate tone and making the personality of the poet even more elusive. From now on, we are never really sure whether Donnelly is hiding his poetic self or his public self. Yet it is often that very quality – what GS Fraser has called "elusive honesty" – which often seems his most attractive characteristic.[34]

But if the conflicts of the street gave his writing strength, they continued to make demands on his day-to-day life also. In addition to their work in the slums, another important Congress battle-front was the picket line. Many Dublin employers were paying wages which were well below subsistence level. One article in the *Republican Congress* newspaper records a wage of five shillings for forty hours of work. Manual workers in Dublin's factories had almost no legal rights. Moreover, memories of the defeat of the great strike of 1913 were still fresh in the minds of workers and employers alike. Having crushed working-class defiance on that occasion, the authorities were determined not to lose their grip now. In most workplaces, even the suggestion of forming a union was punishable by immediate dismissal. Charles Donnelly became involved with the Congress pro-Union campaign and was arrested, released, and arrested again.

By now, in the summer of 1934, Donnelly's university career was about to end. He had repeated his first year arts examinations and failed once more. In any case, the threats and abuse he continued to receive from fascist-inspired members of the college Christian Union was becoming too much even for him.

There has been a suggestion, in Michael O'Riordan's lively book, *Connolly Column*, that Donnelly was expelled from UCD because of his activities in the Student Vanguard.[35] There is certainly no evidence for this, and, indeed, it seems unlikely that the college authorities would have been even aware of what was basically a student debating society.

A far more likely cause for official concern would have been Donnelly's arrest and imprisonment for two weeks in July, 1934, on charges arising from his role in picketing a Dublin city bakery. I suppose it is possible that as a trouble-making Communist Donnelly might have been refused permission to return to college for the new term. But in any case, he did not want to go back. Those days were over now. Charles Donnelly traded the libraries of UCD for street politics in the slums of Dublin. He was, by now, a full time radical activist.

For Donnelly's father, the arrest and jail sentence were a bitterly predictable blow. He felt that he had done his best. Dogged by worries about his children, trying to survive in an unhappy and unwanted marriage, tolerant up to a point of what he saw as

Charles's stupid whims and even his disastrous university career, he felt that he was now being asked to sanction his son's contempt for the law and for civilised values. They quarrelled bitterly, and, according to George Gilmore and others, Charles was told to leave the family home.

He spent his nights sleeping under newspapers on the park benches of Dublin. He slept in the streets, and on the floors of friends' lodgings whenever he could. He became a homeless person.

He became a part of the very underclass whose rights he had fought so hard to defend.

CHAPTER FOUR

Friends remember what happened to Charles Donnelly at this time. They remember that he was short of money, depressed, anxious. They remember that he was cold and hungry and sick. The son of a wealthy man, he often had no money for food or clothes. But despite all of this, his compassion for the poor and his devotion to their cause became more committed all the time.

He taught himself the art of political oratory. From the street corners of Dublin he spoke about Socialism, about the possibility of a better world, to men and women who could barely read or write. He told people that they could band together to find decency. He told them that the rich were rich because they were poor. He quoted Larkin. "The great are only great because we are on our knees," he would say. "Let us arise!"

His love affair with Cora Hughes continued during this worst of times, but it was constantly under terrible strain. Her parents continued to try to stop her from seeing him. The lack of personal acceptance from his comrades still troubled and hurt him, but he tried to forget about it and to steel himself for the revolution that he believed was coming.

One month after Donnelly's release from Mountjoy Jail the Republican Congress met, in full session, for the first time. It was already beset by problems. As the delegates filed past the hordes of religious protestors and into Rathmines Town Hall, nobody really knew what political significance the new movement would have. As a loose united front campaigning on local workers' issues it had been making some kind of progress. But when the time came to decide on policy positions there was the usual outbreak of intense confusion, mistrust and disunity which only the Left seems able to manage.

Broadly, Congress activists fell into two categories. This division emerged early when an organisation committee was formed and promptly split. George Gilmore recalled later:

This cleavage ... as to the form the Republican Congress was to take and the manner of campaigning that it ought to pursue ... was expressed directly in rival resolutions on organisation – one in favour of the formation of a new political party, the other calling for united front activities – and was indicated also in two rival policy resolutions (on the nature of Republicanism) which, though not formally linked to the two organisational resolutions, embodied the theories on which they were based.[36]

The minority resolution calling for the establishment of a united front, supported by Gilmore, Ryan, Peadar O'Donnell, and most of the younger activists like Donnelly and Cora Hughes, was narrowly carried. The minority resolution on Republicanism, which outlined the real political objectives of the Congress, was also carried. There was uproar. The fact that these motions were carried so narrowly meant that in effect there would never be a united front. Once again, the Irish Left had done a good job of almost strangling itself in the womb.

Nevertheless, Charles Donnelly was elected a member of the National Executive that supported these two resolutions. The manifesto to which he signed his name was uncompromising in its language and its thinking:

The Republican Congress, rallying centre for mass struggles, capable of smashing imperialist and native exploiters, calls for a UNITED FRONT of working-class and small farmers so that the submerged nation may be roused to free itself, and to free and unite the Irish Republic.[37]

He was twenty years old, part of the leadership of a socialist movement which had as its ultimate aim the destruction of the mechanisms of the state itself and the completion of the Irish revolution. "As usual," one of his comrades recalled, "he took all this with deadly solemnity."

His elevation to the leadership of the campaign had important effects on Donnelly. The following long recollection by George Gilmore is, I think, worth quoting in full:

As he became more involved with the Congress he became more politically mature. Of course, he still read Lenin and Trotsky, but in a new light. He was evolving the view that it was Irish progressives and socialists who held the key to the fight for Irish freedom. Not that he was becoming a bourgeois nationalist, he never did. But he began to read Connolly voraciously, collecting his scattered journalism, attempting a synthesis and a reclamation of Connolly by the left.

In all this he would have been influenced strongly by the Congress, especially veterans of the rising or the Tan war. The other important thing is that people like Charlie were rare in the movement. It was predominantly a genuine working-class small farmer movement from the roots up. Even the IRA men were not in the leadership because of their records, but because of their class and their experience. Of course, I would not advocate theoretical illiteracy, but very many of the Congress men and women were rough diamonds who had lived in poverty or been hounded in and out of jail. They learnt their political theory in prison cells, or on the end of a Blueshirt baton. The theory evolved out of the practice for most of us.

With Charlie of course, it was different. And to an extent it always would have been. He was from a wealthy background, an apolitical family. He had an education and was really an intellectual – all of which meant that there was occasionally a suspicion of him, at best a feeling that he needed the corners knocked off him, as it were.

Well, the Congress certainly did that. He threw himself into it, organising tenants and workers, getting attacked by the fascists. I would say that ordinarily it is impossible for a member of the bourgeoisie to change colour politically. To really feel and experience the depth of the rotteness of capitalism ... I mean, the sheer crude savagery of it. That emotional response. Without that, socialism is glib and paternalistic. My point is that Charlie found this out through his work with us in the Congress. He definitely did have these romantic ideas about the glorious martyr-like working-class while he was in college. And in my view that tendency in him was aggravated by a purely academic understanding of Marxism. But he soon found out that actually working with members of that class who were poor and dirty, who reeked of their poverty, who lived in rat-infested hovels ... well, it was a long way from UCD. And he is honestly the only middle-class person I ever met, with the possible exception of Cora Hughes, who ever fully realised this.[38]

After the so-called "Majority Resolution" had been

passed, Congress members returned to their branches and campaigns, distributing their pamphlets and their newspaper, involving themselves in strikes, organising meetings which were often broken up by policemen or young fascists wielding clubs and knives.

Charles Donnelly became an important contributor to the *Republican Congress* newspaper, but he was never again to write the abstract theoretical essays of his early days in UCD. His journalism became more involved, pragmatic and agitational, reflecting the fact that the Congress was a Leftist movement with clear political objectives and a planned set of strategies to achieve them.

Republican Congress was one of the best political newspapers ever produced in Ireland. Despite incredible difficulties, lack of staff and money, reluctant printers, a newsagents' ban, not to mention the political tensions in the organisation itself, the newspaper was published regularly for two years. The design and layout was basic but efficient, the articles informed and surprisingly well-written. In addition to regular features, the paper carried reports, analyses and personal testimonies from Congress members and supporters. Donnelly rapidly became something of a journalistic all-rounder. He wrote articles on tenant strikes, the land war, the British royal family, international events, book reviews, news reports. "When you needed something done in a hurry" George Gilmore said, "you got Charlie Donnelly."

Donnelly's particular speciality, however, lay in writing about current events and putting them into a theoretical framework. In the best of his articles theory and actuality seem to blend, the synthesis of the two leading to a logical conclusion, the political action which should be taken. In much the same way that he organised his poetry, his journalism also centres around tensions, contradictions and clever resolutions.

Here, he is writing about de Valera's economic plan for Ireland:

De Valera was adopted by the industrialists as their new representative. In de Valera's administration the policy of Griffith has been worked out to its conclusion – and the conclusion of the self-sufficiency programme is a search for foreign markets for the products of Irish industry.

What is the meaning of this? That industry is being built, not on the firm foundation of a free and prosperous peasantry, but on the foundation of an impoverished peasantry and primitive agricultural methods. It means that in failing to see that the land war was not yet over and in failing to give a lead to the land struggles, Griffith failed to lay a foundation for his policy.[39]

Having established the theoretical framework, Donnelly moves on, arguing for his politics with a new found passionate style:

Today men in Connacht struggle to wring a living out of land so shallow that the furrow must be cut wider than the ridge. Unfortunate farmers in the Gaeltacht attempt to create soil out of the unstripped bog by treating it with limestone. The technical level of Irish agriculture is the lowest in Europe. Meanwhile – while the farmers scratch the soil with century-old implements in competition with modern mechanised farming – the factories, which should be harnessed to the production of the means for up-to-date farming, produce clothing, pottery, aluminium, to flood the markets of the world!

Creating his synthesis, Donnelly proposes a course of action:

Self-sufficiency is an impossible ideal for Ireland. But de Valera's system of industrial production, based on an impoverished countryside, for foreign markets which have yet to be found – this is suicidally impossible ... An alternative perspective of industrial development can be offered by labour and Republicanism. A programme of the linking of industry and agriculture, the employment of the factories to supply the mechanical and chemical sinews for up-to-date farming, the completion of land division on a non-compensation basis, the removal of financial burdens from the small farmers, the development of cooperative farming, rate and annuity relief for the small farmers, progressive system of taxation, ranch division without compensation, minimum wages for agricultural workers.[40]

Stylistically, then, this is a typical Donnelly article from this period. But what of its actual politics? Reflecting the fact the Congress was essentially a united front movement, the article eschews wearisome Leftist dogma. Each policy is argued for on its merits, and not on undergraduate notions of ideological purity. This new pragmatism made Donnelly's politics more finely tuned and specific. In an organisation of very disparate elements, held together only by its programme, this was absolutely necessary. George Gilmore confirms this:

You see, we were forced to think and write in clear terms, saying exactly what our policies were and how they could be achieved – not only for organisational reasons but for political ones also. Activists found that many of the workers and small farmers were genuinely sick of rhetorical politicians. The people would ask us exactly what we meant in our objectives, what did this workers' Republic mean, what did we mean by connecting their own struggles with the Republican question, what was the nature of that connection, exactly how could we organise politically to further their demands within the system while simultaneously organising to overthrow that system. Charlie had the energy as well as the intellect to make these connections and explain them clearly.[41]

Other particularly impressive articles include "Reformism, Insurrection and Revolution", in the 5 October, 1935 number of the paper. Again Donnelly blends his theoretical objection to the insurrectionism of the IRA with practical argument, thus defending the work of the Congress. Answering accusations of parliamentarianism levelled at the movement, Donnelly is trenchant:

Let us be clear as to the extent of the revolution which we wish to carry out: we wish to take economic power out of the hands of one class and place it in those of another. Our difference with those who accuse us of parliamentarianism is that we have so little use for parliament and the existing state, and visualise its overthrow in so real a way that we see the necessity for replacing this state by another state.

Granted – and everything proves that it would be impossible – that by a conspiratorial rising we could capture power. Unless this rising took place in the heart of a rising people, and unless the working people were prepared and organised to carry out the work previously done by the state and the class overthrown by the revolution, power could not be retained for a month and certainly no changeover from the capitalist system to a workers' state could be effected.[42]

Once again, Donnelly establishes the theoretical background and moves with potent effect to a catalogue of specifics:

What would be the tasks with which the revolutionary government would be faced? The tasks of dividing the ranchlands, of taking the more important industries out of the hands of the capitalists, and of establishing some means of compulsion over the smaller employers, of organising the distribution of farm products among the town workers and the distribution of the products of industry in the countryside. It would have to create machinery for controlling production in accordance with the requirements of the country, take control of the banks and adapt the money system to this end ... The majority of the factories would have closed down, the streets would be thronged with idle workers, the old civil service, postal and telegraphic officials and probably the official labour leaders [would be] antagonists ... What machinery would the revolution have at its disposal for restoring order to this chaos, for even keeping production running to avoid a famine let alone organising production for use instead of for profit? Would the army take control of the factories, the postal and telegraphic system, supervise prices to prevent profiteering and organise distribution? Of course it would not.[43]

Following this list of potential disasters, Donnelly deals the final blow to his opponents and outlines his own answers to these questions:

Here is the real meaning of armed insurrection without mass revolution. These revolutionaries who deny the necessity for political work and mass organisation and agitation deny the necessity for organising the people to replace the old state by the new workers' state. They do not visualise the replacement of the capitalist state by a workers' state, however much they talk, and talk sincerely, about the workers' Republic. In reality they would not destroy the old state at all, they would merely take control of it, and to take control of it by armed insurrection is not one bit more a revolution than to take control of it by a parliamentary majority.

We must have in our hands machinery by which we can run the economic life of this country. This machinery cannot be created on the morning of the revolution. It must be created before the revolution rises on the horizon, in the daily struggles of the small farmers against the burden of the banks, high prices, rates and annuities, of the landless men for the land.[44]

Some of the predictions of future political events in Donnelly's *Republican Congress* articles have turned out to be remarkably and tragically accurate. He was correct about the miserable failure of de Valera's economic policy. In 1933 he was writing that there would be another world war within five years, and that England and Italy would be enemies in that war. Based on a shrewd analysis of the ultra-nationalist direction in which the IRA was moving, he predicted that in that war these pseudo-revolutionaries would attempt an alliance with fascism.

But not much of Charles Donnelly's time was spent on political speculation. There was always a need for action also. On 14 September 1934, he was arrested once again, this time for picketing the Bridewell Jail where some Congress members had been imprisoned. He refused to pay his fine, only to find that it had already been paid, anonymously, on his behalf, probably by a member of his family. Donnelly was dismayed about this. According to friends, he actually wanted to be arrested again as he entertained romantic notions about the political credibility which would result from this.

He was soon to fulfil his ambition. Early in the new year, twenty five congress members were picketing a shop when the police arrived to break things up. Donnelly made a rather feeble attempt to head-butt a policeman. He and Cora and all of the other picketers were arrested. On 12 January 1935 he was charged with assembly so as to cause obstruction, besetting a shop, threatening behaviour, and the almost admirably inclusive "threatening, insulting and abusive words and behaviour". He was given the choice of a five pound ten shilling fine, or a month in jail. This time nobody turned up to pay. Donnelly made a speech refusing to recognise the authority of the court and was duly imprisoned. As he was led away by two policemen he was ecstatic. In Mountjoy Jail he wrote "The Flowering Bars".

After sharp words from the fine mind,
protest in court,
the intimate high head constrained,
strait lines of prison, empty walls,
a subtle beauty in a simple place.

But Donnelly's elation was short lived. His rough living had worn him down, and in his cell in Mountjoy he was frequently sick and depressed. The glamour of being a proletarian hero was, presumably, not much of a consolation as the weeks of his sentence dragged by. He was separated from Cora, who had been imprisoned herself, despite personal appeals from her father to his old school friend, de Valera. He received very few visitors. Most of his Congress comrades, with the exception of

George Gilmore, were too busy to visit him, and would probably, as Gilmore quipped, not have gone within a hundred miles of Mountjoy unless they were in handcuffs. None of his college friends came. Neither did his family. He was not allowed to have books. It must have been a very forceful lesson in the loneliness of the hero's lot.

Things were about to get worse, however. While Donnelly was busily playing the role of jailed political martyr he received some tragic news from home. His young stepbrother, Philip, had died.

Guilty and despairing, Donnelly decided he had taken enough. He made up his mind to get out of Ireland. Immediately following his release, on 12 February 1935, he left for London.

It is perhaps important to point out that he did not leave for the reasons that have led countless Irish writers into exile. He did not discover, like Joyce, that the shortest way to Tara was via Holyhead. All Holyhead offered to Charles Donnelly is what it offers to most people. A train to a place where they can survive. He could not afford the luxury of the exiled artist's pose. He left his country because he was despairing, poor, homeless and unemployed. He left Ireland for the same reasons people still leave it today.

CHAPTER FIVE

When Charles Donnelly arrived in London he was pale, thin and ill. He went straight to the Kilburn flat of an old Trinity College friend, Leslie Daiken, and he asked for a place to sleep. "I just had to get out of that bloody place," he explained, dismissively, "it's hard to stand the stupidity any longer."

For the first few weeks he said little to Daiken about his reasons for fleeing the country. But eventually he confided that he had never really wanted to leave. He missed his friends, Frank Ryan and George Gilmore. He missed Cora most of all. He spoke about her very frequently to the new friends he was to meet in London. He was "overwhelmingly in love", Daiken recalled, and very lonely without her.

Yet, paradoxically, it was in this strange new city that Charles Donnelly was to find something like real happiness for the first time in his life. He loved London, its street life and its colour. He felt that he belonged there. He continued to work for the Republican Congress: he became chief organiser of its London branch. But he broadened out his interests and his activities. The diffident young man with the bookish mind even began to enjoy himself.

Daiken recalls the endless round of political meetings and social events he attended with Charles Donnelly. There were long nights drinking beer in pubs, and coffee in Lyons Corner Houses, arguing about writers and ideologies. There were fascinating, committed men and women. There was above all a sense, Daiken recalls, that the Left was on the rise, that capitalism was in its death throes, that a new and humane order was coming. He was tragically wrong, of course. But London in the mid thirties must have seemed a maze of desire and possibility.

Daiken's unpublished memoir of his friend is in the possession of the Donnelly family. His colourful prose conveys something of the excitement of the times:

Those were heroic days of dream and struggle. We were one of the steam-hammers. A job was only a meal ticket until the whole rotten sytem would crack up ... Our household was crazy and Chekhovian but addicted to hope ... [Donnelly] liked browsing at the bookstalls and was a regular caller at Joe Fowler's bookshop at Saint Giles ... Life was one long continuum of agit prop ... His animated, goblinesque little face recurring as though in the impressionistic flashes of a film, over a sea of other faces, at street corners, market places, halls, club rooms, Hyde Park – that mecca of most Irish commemoration rallies, next to the public figures on gala platforms. Even at the ceilidhe we ran in aid of branch funds, he continued to find an unobtrusive platform. He did not dance.

Money was never plentiful but casual work was easy enough to find. Donnelly did the usual round of low-paid, part-time immigrant work in bars and cafes. Eventually he found better paid work at an international news agency with an Irish friend, the writer, Montague Slater. But it was the street life of London that really began to beguile him. Daiken tells us:

In poverty or plenty he always seemed preoccupied with thought, action, never his stomach or a bed. Class never entered into his respect for intellect, most

*immense of his enthusiasms. There was no casual
adventure that excited him so much as having held
conversation with a knowledgable person ... he talked
the poetry and pathology of love better than any
Proust, comparing notes and subtleties, analogy-
mongering and rhapsodising over the discovery of a
coincidence with an ecstatic chuckle. Though hungry
as hell he would buy a package of good cigarettes and
a book before investing in an anaemic meal – even
when he drew good wages. A cafe was merely an
opportune theatre for enjoying books and tobacco and
people, and brave earnest talk.*

While in London Donnelly wrote for a variety of left-
wing magazines, including *Reynolds News*,
International Press Correspondence, and the official
newspaper of the Communist Party, *The Daily Worker*.
The scope of his interest and ability is astonishing for
one of his youth. There are articles on all aspects of
Irish history and politics, economics, philosophy,
literature. There are book reviews, short stories and
poems. He lectured on Marxism and Irish history to
trade union groups, and he began to write an
extensive critical biography of James Connolly, some
notes of which still survive.

Perhaps most prophetically, he developed a keen
interest in the study of military strategy, and he
contributed a thesis on the tactics of the Spanish
peninsular wars, for which he was highly commended,
to the distinguished military historian Captain Basil
Liddel-Hart.

None of Donnelly's writings on military strategy were
published, and so we must rely on the original
manuscripts for information. Some of these papers are
untidy and illegible, making accurate description
difficult. It is possible to isolate with certainty only some
of the areas of the science of war which intrigued him.

One of his principal military interests was in the tactical operations of guerrilla armies. He wrote several versions of a paper on that topic, and in one of these he explains his interest. The Left, he argues, had always been weak on military strategy. Although civil war had been taken for granted as an inescapable stage in the development of socialism in most countries, very little study had been devoted to its conditions and conduct. The future of Europe would be decided by war, he added, prophetically, and Fascism would not be defeated by correct politics alone.

For Donnelly, military theory was to be studied for very practical reasons. Revolutionary leaders had never done this. Too much thought had been given to political theory, and not enough to the science of action. Even important revolutionaries like Bela Kun in Hungary had fallen into this trap. More importantly, for Donnelly, so had James Connolly.

In a series of articles on insurrectionary warfare, Donnelly analyses Connolly's military mistakes. He takes as his starting point a series of eight Connolly articles on military strategy, published in the *Workers' Republic* paper in 1915. These were short analyses by Connolly of the Moscow insurrection of 1905, the Tyrol insurrection of 1809, the Belgian Revolution, the Battle of the Alamo, the Paris Revolution of 1830, the French Revolution of 1848 and the Battle of Lexington, at the beginning of the American Revolution. They had been written with the purpose of condensing the lessons of military strategy used in these conflicts into a broad sketch on insurrectionary warfare to be used by Citizens' Army members. A handbook of street fighting, in effect. Donnelly made it his task to correct Connolly's errors and he began to read widely in the area of military history.

He continued to write about contemporary ideologies, also, and Charles Donnelly's observations on the politics of Fascism are among the most interesting and tragically accurate of his political writings. "Fascism" he had written, in UCD, "is the despairing attempt of capitalism to maintain its power, and the property relations in which its power is expressed, at a time when these relations are no longer compatible with human progress".[45] The ideology which was to claim his life was one that he understood clearly and prophetically.

Writing in a book review for *Republican Congress*, Donnelly relates his theory of Fascist tactics to the contemporary political situation in Ireland:

One of the most obvious characteristics of the Fascist method is its attempt to get a mass basis for the Capitalist policy, its systematic use of demagogy. Palme Dutt gives a section of the book to "Demagogy as a Science", opened, very aptly, by the following quotation from Al Capone, the American gangster chief:

"Bolshevism is knocking at our gates. We can't afford to let it in. We have got to organise ourselves against it, and put our shoulders together and hold fast. We must keep America whole and safe and unspoiled. We must keep the worker away from red literature and red ruses; we must see that his mind remains healthy."

Widening his perspective, Donnelly makes a telling point:

Among the items on the Fascist programme in Italy were: the land for the peasants, transference of control of industry to syndicates of workers and technicians; abolition of monarchy, senate and

76

nobility, and creation of a Republic. Similarly in Ireland the Blueshirt Fascists have started a "No Rent" campaign with the object of winning the support of the small farmers, and an attempt has already been made in Dublin to use the discontent of the Tramway workers with the Trade Union bureaucrats to form a Fascist trade union.

These events show us that in Ireland we may very well take seriously Palme Dutt's warning that Fascism comes when "owing to the failure of decisive working class leadership to rally all discontented strata, the discredited old regime is able to draw to its support under specious quasi-revolutionary slogans all the wavering elements ... and on the very basis of the crisis and discontent which should have given allies to the revolution, build up the forces of reaction in the form of Fascism."[46]

Donnelly continues by arguing that the fight against Fascism is not a defensive struggle for democracy, but an intrinsic part of the advance to socialism.

The above analysis of Fascism is important, I think. After all, it was precisely through the appropriation of working class leadership that Fascism came to power during the doomed years of Germany's Weimar Republic. Franco used the same methods in Spain. In more recent times, a great problem for the Left has been that extreme Right movements – the National Front in Britain and France, the Ku Klux Klan, the Afrikaaner Nationalists, the Nicaraguan Contras – have been almost exclusively working-class in their membership. These organisations are held together by reaction and bigotry, whipped up by Fascist-style leaders, for their own ends. The only time that the world socialist movement has acted with political acumen on this problem was ironically during the decade in which Fascism was to take root all over Europe. This problem is one that still goes to the heart of the national question in Ireland. One of the few people in Irish politics to have ever proposed radical political solutions was Charles Donnelly. These solutions were proposed sixty years ago by the men and women of the Republican Congress, non-sectarian revolutionaries who have been conveniently pushed into the dark corners of history by a version of Republicanism which is a travesty of that ideology.

After some months Donnelly broke his silence and began to correspond with members of his family back in Dublin. Shortly after this his brother Tom came to London and moved in with Charles, Leslie Daiken, an ex-IRA man Sean Mulgrew and the odd assortment of expatriate Irishmen who drifted sporadically in and out of Daiken's shabby flat. Tom Donnelly soon found a job at a factory in Acton, West London, and he and Charles went to live there, in a small flat in Chaucer Road. But the Donnelly brothers maintained close links with Daiken, and Charles continued his writing and his political work.

Daiken was at that time editing a monthly magazine called *Irish Front*. Donnelly took half the burden from him. For twenty three numbers they continued to edit it jointly, although some issues are written almost entirely by Donnelly.

Irish Front was the London version of *Republican Congress*. It carried shortened versions of articles from the Irish paper, and was an effective way of circumventing importation difficulties. Because it was produced in London, it gave the Congress an opportunity to recruit for members and advertise its meetings there. In addition to the Irish articles, there were pieces dealing with the problems and experiences of the Irish immigrant community. It carried articles in the Irish language (which *Republican Congress* never did) and, indeed, Donnelly's name appears from time to time in its Irish version. The cheaply produced magazine sold well, and Donnelly and Daiken's manifestoes, analyses and calls to action were effective in keeping the Irish community in touch with its own and with international political issues.

Donnelly became more busy all the time. A group called the Labour Research Bureau commissioned him to prepare a survey on Irish banking, which is detailed, cogent and astute. His letters back to Dublin reveal a new pragmatism. He writes about working with Liddel-Hart on a Fabian Research Bureau committee to draw up a statement on Britain's "defence" needs, adding that this seems odd work for a socialist, but necessary, in order to make the Labour Party more popular and electable. Socialists, he argued, must be strong on the traditional issues of the right. They must not allow the forces of conservatism to steal the high moral ground.

During Donnelly's stay in London, several Dublin friends and members of the family came to visit him, including Cora Hughes and his father, with whom some sort of reconciliation had been made. Another visitor was his young brother Joe.

Through his work on *Irish Front*, Donnelly came into contact with the League Against Imperialism, a small United Front organisation led by anti-imperialist rebels from all over the British empire and colonies. By now he was a very effective orator, precise, unemotional yet extremely powerful, and he became a much sought-after speaker on Irish matters. He spoke all over Britain, and, through the

79

league, became a supporter of a wide variety of Republican, Communist and anti-racist movements, particularly those concerned with China, Cyprus and the African countries.

But perhaps ironically, it was only after he had left his home country that Charles Donnelly began really to understand its political and historical nuances. It was in London that he wrote a thirty page pamphlet called "The Irish Republic at the Crossroads", a cogent socio-economic essay dealing with Irish politics from the founding of the state in 1922 to the birth of the Republican Congress and the election of 1934. The following outline is necessarily sketchy, but it gives some idea of Donnelly's views of the history of his own time.

The piece argues that the Fianna Fáil government of 1935 occupied exactly the same position as that of Collins and Griffith in 1922. Fianna Fáil claimed that it was leading the fight against Imperial domination, that it was advancing towards an Irish Republic by economic development. Militant Republicans, however, insisted that the government was carrying out its policies solely in the interests of the Free State capitalists who had betrayed that very Republic in 1922.

In so far as this policy involved a struggle against Imperialism, Donnelly contended, the government should be supported by the progressive movement. But, he added, Fianna Fáil's policies could never lead to real independence, and the hardship which these measures were imposing on working people were isolating those people from Republicanism under false pretences.

Donnelly located this phenomenon in recent history. The Cosgrave government had been afraid of the dislocation which a change in the economic structure of the country would cause. It had also been worried by the popular swing to Republicanism during the early years of the state. Its main concern had become the agricultural sector of the economy. This had led to a clash of interests between the wealthy agricultural exporters in the Free State and the industrial capitalist class. By 1932, this conflict had become a crisis; the British market for Free State agricultural produce could only be maintained at the expense of industrial development. As a corollary, industrial development could only be carried on through an economic policy which involved the destruction of the agricultural export trade. This had been an element in the Fianna Fáil victory of 1932. Following that success, the new government had initiated an era of attempted reconstruction, of which the economic war with Britain was the chief aspect. What Fianna Fáil had had in mind was "controlled capitalism" as opposed to a pure market economy. Hiding behind its populist nationalism Fianna Fáil had been propogating the theory that its economic ideas were not those of foreign capitalism. Donnelly quotes a government policy statement:

[Our] policy is a new policy. The philosophy behind it runs counter to the prevailing economic philosophy in a great part of the world. For generations our economists and industrialists have been educated in the old system. The government wants them to accept the new.[47]

Using profit figures from major industries, Donnelly exposes this as a specious lie. He goes on to point out that the real brunt of the economic war was being borne by the small farmers and peasant proprietors and that it "struck the capitalists only in the last instance." Because all of this eventually affected purchasing power, the home market for Irish produce contracted. But this contraction was accompanied by an expansion of industry, the contraction maintaining itself because industry was the last economic centre to feel the contraction.

In the light of this economic pressure, the fight against Imperialism by Fianna Fáil would be sustained only to the point where it would be consistent with the interests of the capitalist class. This interest was expressed through organisations like the Federation of Irish Industries and the Industrial Development Associations which had formed all over the country during the early thirties. Donnelly argues that the trend of Fianna Fáil's economic policy substantiated James Connolly's criticism that capitalism in Ireland could only be developed through intolerable conditions for the working class. "Low wages and a high rate of exploitation" Donnelly maintains, "are as necessary to the development of the capitalist economy in Ireland in the twentieth century as is protection, and vigorous government assistance to industry. Consequently, the big obstacle to the capitalists has been the trade union organisations". Therefore, it was necessarily a part of the government's policy of industrial development to lead the employers' struggles against the unions.

All of this made a nonsense of the nationalist claim that Ireland could be self-sufficient. The tariff war and suppression of workers and small farmers would result in the eventual deconstruction of that policy. The resulting economic weakness of the state would make it easier for Britain to maintain its economic hold on Ireland in the future, and possibly lead to a situation where Ireland could one day be used as a war base. So, quite ironically, the nationalists of Fianna Fáil, far from being Republicans, were not even real nationalists. Caught up in their own political contradictions they were mortgaging the future of the state, and eliminating the possibility of that state ever becoming a nation, except under the kind of imperialist terms which would prevent it ever becoming a real Republic.

As a detailed analysis of the shambles of post-revolutionary Ireland, Donnelly's piece is thought-provoking and powerful.

In the libraries of London, Charles Donnelly was now reading more than ever before. Gibbon, James Connolly, Thomas MacDonagh, Shelley, Eliot, Yeats and, always, his beloved Keats. George Gilmore told me about a passionate letter he had received from Charles, in the spring of 1936. In it, he spoke about uniting politics and poetry, about, as George told me, "reading Shelley in a political context and Connolly in a literary one." He exchanged new poems and ideas with friends, and wrote hundreds of pages of political work.

His journalism became more vivid all the time. He progressed from writing for small publications like *Irish Front*, to the influential and widely-respected *Left Review*. One of his most important pieces for that magazine is the article on Connolly and Roger Casement in the July 1936 number.

The two-section article was written under the joint by-line of Charles Donnelly and Ajax, a nom-de-plume of his friend, Montague Slater. The first section is an imagined dialogue between Roger Casement and George Bernard Shaw, wherein Shaw is suggesting lines of defence Casement might adopt in his imminent trial. Slater wrote Shaw's part and Donnolly wrote Casement's.

SHAW – (for the defence): The fact that I served England well enough to have my services publicly acknowledged and especially rewarded shows that I have no quarrel with England except the political quarrel which England respects and applauds in Poland, Italy, Belgium, in short, in every country except those conquered and denationalised by England herself.

CASEMENT – Yes I have. I deny "England's" claim to India and Egypt even as I deny her claim to Ireland – on the very ground that what I claim for one country I should never withhold from others, and not aid them, too, to obtain. I am not only an Irish nationalist, but an anti-imperialist.

SHAW – (for the defence): If you persist in treating me as an Englishman you bind yourselves to hang me as a traitor before the eyes of the world. Now, as a simple matter of fact, I'm neither an Englishman nor a traitor: I am an Irishman captured in a fair attempt to achieve the independence of my country, and you can no more deprive me of the honours of the position than the abominable cruelties inflicted 600 years ago on William Wallace in this city ... My neck is at your service if it amuses you to break it; my honour and reputation are beyond your reach. I ask for no mercy, pardon or pity.

CASEMENT – Shaw's version is all right: but he does not understand one tenth-part of the issue the Crown had in view. They are not after me – except in so far as they have to keep in with public feeling. They are out to befoul Germany first of all: to show up the "German plot" and "Clan-ni-Gail" plot and then to belittle me personally and point to the trio as fine guides and helpers for the Irish people. The reaction is to have this effect – glorification of goodwill of the Irish fighters who fought and died in Ireland – misled and deceived by Germany and by me – but contempt and scorn for those who misled them and later (in the aftermath of a hopeless delusion) to get all the Irish Nationalists into the war on England's side, and satisfy "legal Irish Nationality" by some promise of Home Rule – that nauseous fraud – when the common enemy, Germany, is beaten.[48]

The second section of the article is Donnelly's "defence of Connolly's leading of the Easter Rising, from the point of view of Socialism and Internationalism." This section uses material from Donnelly's research into his proposed biography of Connolly. The point of the article is that while Shaw was "a good nationalist", Casement was anti-imperialist, and that James Connolly took the next step in Irish politics by becoming an internationalist.

Donnelly argues to confirm Casement's prediction of the shunning of the military leaders, especially Connolly, who was denounced as a bourgeois nationalist by broad sections of the Left, and as a crazed adventurer by the British Labour Party. He identifies in Labour politician Tom Johnson's stupified quote on the Easter Rising – "the psychology of it all is a mystery to me" – an epitaph for the political collapse of Labourism. He goes on to associate Connolly with Lenin and Rosa Luxembourg, arguing that long before the outbreak of the First World War he had uncovered the theoretical veins indicative of the Revolutionary Socialism that were to cohere in the foundation of the Third International. He gives an economic analysis – that in the barren soil of Irish economic life, attenuated by imperialist abuse and maladministration, the kind of distributionist Socialism espoused by the British Left was a nonsense. Ireland was a link in a chain of imperial relations, whereas England's economy was at the centre of an imperial system. As such, distributory reform could not be a solution, or even a tactic, for the Irish Left; what was required was a revolution in international relations. Connolly and Casement had each seen this, he argues. This was what led to "the essentially internationalist character of the Revolutionary Nationalism" for which they fought.

Donnelly insists that the 1916 insurrection must be seen as "a rising against the war", and not as a retreat from Socialism on Connolly's part. For Connolly, he maintains, the attainment of Socialism was not a process of logical development towards a better order, but a war of opposing forces. The national struggle emerged directly from this war and was a political condition of it. But it was a real war, demanding leadership of a national revolutionary movement that was potentially and rationally an ally of the Left.

The Irish Socialist Movement, he argues, was a predestined casualty in a vanguard revolutionary action. The time had come to reclaim that internationalist strand of Irish radical thought and put it to political use once again.

London had been good for Charles Donnelly. He was by now a sophisticated and rigorous political thinker. He had moved a long way from the naïve idealism of his university writings. His political experience had matured him, and, in the space of a very few years, brought him to new conceptions of the possibility of a more humane world.

But during the summer of 1936, a conflict was brewing that would test those conceptions to the limit. Far away from the colourful world of alternative London cafe society, a shadow was slowly spreading across Europe.

CHAPTER SIX

In Spain, on 17 July, 1936, a rebel faction within the army rose up against the Popular Front government of Leftist Republicans, communists and socialists. Three days later a counter-coup began. Workers, peasants and intellectuals who supported the Republic formed militia units to defend the elected government. These were organised and led by the trade unions and the Communist Party. A violent clash was inevitable. This was the beginning of the Spanish Civil War.

A few very brief comments on the origin of the war are required, in order to put Donnelly's support for the Spanish Republic into context. From the abdication of the king in April 1931 until 1933, a coalition Republican-socialist government held power in Spain. One of the most important challenges for the new government was to end the long-held and frequently abused political power of the Catholic church. The coalition had gone a long way towards doing this when it was replaced by a centre-right government in 1933. The following year, armed insurrections broke out in Catalonia and Asturia, and were brutally crushed by the army. Arising out of all this, the Popular Front was formed, and won power in the elections of February, 1936. Almost immediately, an ultra-right wing element in the army began to organise. They were led by General Francisco Franco, and backed by the church and the wealthy. In July 1936 they tried to take Spain back from its people. They were a fascist army, fighting a fascist cause.

All over Europe the election of the Popular Front had been hailed as an enormous victory for the Left. The progressive movement in Ireland, such as it was, had particular reasons for optimism. After all, here was a poor, predominantly rural country with a powerful Catholic church which had nevertheless opted for social democracy. The parallels seemed obvious. For people like Donnelly and his political associates, this was the first victory against Fascism in Europe. There were already fascist governments in Germany, Italy, Hungary, Greece and Portugal. Even in liberal democracies like Britain and Ireland there were significant ultra-Right movements. Since the beginning of the decade the Left had been on the retreat. The accession of the Front to power in Spain meant that for the first time in years there was hope for democratic Socialism.

The Franco-led coup brought a wave of international outrage. Socialist and intellectual organisations condemned the uprising, as did a handful of brave churchmen and women. Leftist writers in England were particularly vocal. A group of them, led by the poet Stephen Spender, organised a questionnaire to be sent to as many prominent writers as possible, canvassing opinion on the war. The answers were later published by *Left Review* in a pamphlet called "Writers Take Sides". The vast majority of writers and artists supported the Spanish Republic and condemned Franco. Of them all, Samuel Beckett's terse reply – ¡UPTHEREPUBLIC! – was perhaps the most memorable. Several of the writers in this collection were actually to go to fight in Spain themselves, John Cornford, Ralph Fox and Hugh MacDiarmaid among them. This was the era above all others in the twentieth century when artists realised, in Auden's words, that "poetry makes nothing happen", that words are not enough in the battle against injustice.

In London, Charles Donnelly became completely absorbed by the Spanish conflict. He was so preoccupied that he could not sleep or work. He began to argue with his friends that it was time for artists to stop talking and take their part in the physical battle against Fascism, if only because they would be amongst its first victims if it triumphed. Hitler was waging war against German artists, and the great Lorca was already dead.

The Spanish government and international communist parties formed the International Brigades in late 1936 to capitalise on this widespread opposition to Franco. Over the next few years men from all over the world joined the Brigade and went to fight in Spain. Some of the units were small; the Portuguese, South African and Norwegian groups had only a few members. But there were large contingents from the United States and the Soviet Union, fighting side by side. Italians and Germans risked death in their own countries to come and fight Fascism in Spain. Men of all colours and creeds fought together. Every continent, and every European country, was represented in the International Brigade.

From London, Donnelly began sending letters to Frank Ryan and George Gilmore, urging them to make a stand for the Spanish Republic on behalf of the Republican Congress.

The Congress, however, was slow to do this. Ryan was more concerned with a set of more immediate problems, relating to the expulsion of Congress members in the United States from the Clan na Gael movement. In any case, the entire country seemed to be behind Franco. The bishops had allowed churches to be used to collect money for the fascist army: tens of thousands of pounds had been raised. The church, the press and the majority of Irish politicians rushed to Franco's aid. It was a shameful and knowingly dishonest performance. Every distortion possible was tried to squeeze every last penny out of an impoverished people. If you were against Franco, the line went, you were against Christ. The always reliable *Irish Independent* excelled itself. There were "paid agents of Russia ... in every parish in the Free State at present" it reported. There were "40,000 communists in the Free State, prepared to take up arms against God."[49] The same newspaper later editorialised:

On the one side is a so-called government which has abandoned all the functions of government to a Communist junta bent upon the destruction of personal liberty, the eradication of religion, the burning of churches and the wholesale slaughter of the clergy. On the other side are the Patriot army gladly risking liberty, property and life, in the defence of their Faith – fighting the same fight that our Irish ancestors fought for centuries for the same cause.[50]

A pro-Franco pamphlet which sold tens of thousands of copies in Irish churches and schools was just as objective:

Outrages against nuns were many, and too horrible to relate. The complete tale of slaughter of these unresisting religious is known only to Heaven ... The number of priests murdered in this festival of hate was 400 in Barcelona alone. A striking example of the savagery was this: the coffins of nuns were dug up and opened and the bodies of the long dead holy women were put on show in the streets, with hideous results. Dead Carmelite monks were exposed in the same manner ... Dreadful sacrilege was wrought on the Divine Presence on the altar.[51]

90

Feverish support for Franco swept through Ireland that summer. Frank Ryan felt that the Republican Congress simply did not have the resources to fight it. He wrote to Donnelly to explain this.

Donnelly himself had already decided that he was going to fight with the newly formed International Brigade, whatever the Congress said. He came back to Dublin for a brief visit in August 1936, to tell his friends about his decision and try to persuade Ryan personally to change his mind. According to Gilmore, Donnelly quarrelled bitterly with his friend and political senior, accusing him of betraying the internationalist legacy of James Connolly. Ryan answered that while Donnelly had been busy writing accusing letters from London, he had been trying desperately to hold the rapidly weakening Congress together. A compromise was reached when Ryan agreed to send a message of support to the Republicans. For the time being, Donnelly was satisfied, and he spent the rest of his time in Dublin visiting old friends. He saw Gilmore and Cora Hughes.

My information, from what George Gilmore told me directly, is that both George and Cora encouraged him strongly to go and fight against Fascism.

His college friends were certainly less enthusiastic. In the BBC radio documentary on Donnelly's work, Niall Sheridan recalled sadly:

The Spanish Civil War was a very hot issue when we were young, and, of course, we were all on the anti-Franco side. But he [Donnelly] took it even more seriously. This was the showdown between Fascism and the rest. MacDonagh and myself were very saddened, but not surprised, when he came and said he was going to fight against Franco. We spent a whole night trying to convince him that any

91

fool could carry a rifle but that he could do a lot more
important work by staying alive.[52]

Charles Donnelly stayed in Dublin, probably until
October, and he went to see his family several times.
He said nothing about his decision to go and fight.
Before he left, he was to see his old friend, Frank
Ryan, brought irreversibly into the fight with him.

On 20 September, Cardinal McRory, Archbishop of
Armagh, publicly denounced Ryan and the
Republican Congress for sending Donnelly's
suggested message of support to the Spanish
Republicans. This was an evil régime, he said, and
Irish Catholics should have been prepared to send
money for weapons to Franco, or even to go and fight
themselves, if necessary. Ryan, never the most even-
tempered of men, was outraged. In an open letter, he
accused the Cardinal of being in league with "the
forces of Fascism and Imperialism." And in one of the
great put-downs of Irish political history, he added,
"May I assure Your Eminence that as an Irish
Catholic I will take my religion from Rome, but that
as an Irish Republican I will take my politics neither
from Moscow or Maynooth."[53]

Donnelly was absolutely delighted. Ryan and
Gilmore started organising to send a group of Irish
combatants to Spain to help defend the Republic. As
Sean Cronin points out in his authoritative
biography, it was probably the greatest irony of
Ryan's life that the Cardinal was ultimately
responsible for sending him to Spain, thereby saving
the Republican Congress from extinction for several
years. But George Gilmore insists that Charles
Donnelly had an important role in this too:

Although the Congress ultimately failed in its
objectives, chief amongst its achievements was the

leadership of the campaign against Fascism in Spain. That campaign may not have happened were it not for people like Charlie. His main contribution was that he kept pushing us into having an internationalist position. It was interesting because Charlie's political roots were in the Communist Party, whereas ours were in the IRA. Though we wanted a workers' Republic here, we didn't make the connection between Imperialism here and in other countries. And even when it came up in discussions it was sometimes dismissed as being merely theoretical, even by Frank [Ryan] who was later to fight against Fascism in Spain. I suppose it could be said that at the outset we made a political error in not following through Connolly's logic. But because of the pressure of work and imprisonments and dreadful organisational problems, what was happening far away was not always seen as vitally important. But Charlie insisted that it was and he'd quote Connolly chapter and verse to prove it. I think he was the first political theorist to come up with the formulation that Connolly and Casement's nationalism was internationalist, because it was anti-imperialist. Nowadays of course, most sections of the Irish Left would take this for granted. But you have to remember that Charlie Donnelly was saying this back in 1934, when Connolly was still very much a nationalist icon.[54]

On his return to London, Donnelly went to the offices of the Spanish Medical Aid Committee in New Oxford Street. The Irish poet Ewart Milne was working as a volunteer there and he became friendly with Donnelly. In Britain, there had been a great upsurge in support for the Republicans throughout the summer, and the committee had appealed for ambulances and medical supplies to be sent to Spain. Milne and two harassed secretaries had the task of sorting through all this material and arranging for transport. Donnelly offered his assistance, but Milne guessed, correctly, that the young poet wanted to go to Spain himself and was looking for a means to get there.

Milne secured a job for Donnelly, working as a part-time clerk in the Boxers' Union, an organisation which had an office in the same building as the SMAC, and whose secretary was a sympathiser with the Republican cause. It was silently understood that the new clerk might simply not turn up for work one day, and that no questions would be asked about his whereabouts. All of this secrecy was highly necessary. The British government had taken up a so-called "non-intervention" stance on the war, and, although it recognised the legality of the Republican government, it treated the International Brigade as an illegal organisation and regularly set the police on demonstrations of the Arms for Spain movement.

Milne worked long hours at the SMAC office and Donnelly used most of his spare time to help him, sending supplies to the front through Newhaven, Dieppe and Calais. The two men became close very quickly, despite their political differences. The SMAC was an all-party committee very carefully held separate from the International Brigade, which was organised by the Communist Party. Donnelly had secretly joined the Brigade by Christmas, 1936, but he never discussed this openly with Milne. Instead, the two men poets talked about poetry most of the time.

During his last months in London, Donnelly seems to have written at a furious pace, showing his poems to Milne and sending copies of them to friends. Unfortunately, many of these poems have either been lost, or have simply not yet turned up, but some of his best work, including "Poem", dates from this period:

Between rebellion as a private study and the public
Defiance, is simple action only on which will flickers
Catlike, for spring. Whether at nerve-roots is secret
Iron, there's no diviner can tell, only the moment can
show.
Simple and unclear moment, on a morning utterly
different
And under circumstances different from what you'd
expected.

Doctor Valentine Cunningham, the leading authority
on Spanish Civil War writers, has described this as
one of the best poems about the conflict. Here,
sharing Wilfred Owen's suspicion of historiography
but jettisoning that poet's anger, Donnelly comes to a
statement of the anti-heroic that is as subtle as it is
eloquent. In this world, "Poem" argues, death is only
death, no matter what the politicians turn it into.
The rhythm is graceful and simple. There is no
emotion here, not even Owen's deeply human pity.
There is only death. The poetry is in the pitilessness.

Milne remembers that Donnelly was ruthlessly
realistic in his assessment of the war, and deeply
cautious about romanticising it in his poetry. This
particular trap was one into which many of
Donnelly's contemporaries flung themselves during
the "Pink" thirties. Donnelly, however, was more
sensitive to the danger. His one serious altercation
with his friend occurred when Milne commented that
one of Donnelly's poems about Spain was better than
"all that guff about Workers Arise" which was being
published in the little magazines at the time.
Donnelly lost his temper and shouted that he was
not one of those romantic fools who was going to
Spain without even knowing the reality of what they
were doing. He insisted that he had no interest in
adventurism, that he was going to Spain to study the

development of practical military strategy since the Peninsular Wars.

The surviving poems from the last years of Donnelly's life confirm Milne's assertion that he took the dangers of Spain very seriously. The war poems were in fact written before he left for Spain, and in them Donnelly anticipates the process of violent death with a cool objectivity. Probably his best know poem, "The Tolerance of Crows", dates from this period:

Death comes in quantity from solved
Problems on maps, well-ordered dispositions,
Angles of elevation and direction;

This quietly resigned tone is oddly moving, and deeply impressive, especially when so many other poet-volunteers on the Leftist side lapsed into hysteria when faced with the realities of a bloody guerrilla war that had looked so glamorously macho from the vantage point of an Oxford commonroom or a London cafe. Of course, this is understandable in human terms. But it led to some shoddy and clichéd poetry. Hugh MacDiarmaid's outburst on the death of his fellow soldiers makes an interesting comparison with Donnelly's measured coolness:

FASCISTS! You have killed my comrades
And their wives and children!
You have killed them!
It were better that you should rot in your vices,
In the bottomless filth of damnation
And that they should live.[55]

Other poets took refuge in numbingly insipid left wing rhetoric. John Cornford's lines have a hollow ring:

Our fight's not won till all the workers of the world
Stand by our guard on Huesca's plain
Swear that our dead fought not in vain,
Raise the red flag triumphantly
For Communism and for liberty.[56]

WH Auden was to realise in the 1950's that this kind of poetic propaganda ultimately served only to make the fact of death less important than the slogans the volunteers died defending. Compiling a volume of his *Collected Poems* he excised the controversial poem, "Spain", which had spoken of "the necessary murder" of the enemy. If there was one poem he regretted having written, he admitted, this was it.

Charles Donnelly had anticipated these dangers long before. In "The Tolerance of Crows" there are no slogans. The fact of death is all. Donnelly hardly even mentions the enemy, certainly not in MacDiarmaid's fuming terms. His suspicion of propaganda, combined with an implicit anti-war stance in these poems, places Donnelly on a different level, lending his art an almost universal significance. "The Tolerance of Crows" is ultimately a poem about violent death, not about dying for the socialist cause in the Spanish Civil War. There is no sadness, no bitterness, no pity. The only hint of emotion is in Donnelly's childishly disturbed wonder at the banality of death, how it comes to all soldiers as it was to come to him, from the "angles of elevation and direction" of bullets and bombs. By skirting the limits of coldness, "The Tolerance of Crows" achieves an ironically powerful poignancy.

Donnelly told Milne that he was going to risk his life in order to study military strategy, and of course this is complete nonsense. But it reveals how Charles

Donnelly occasionally went too far in his attempts to hold on to his individualism. His dilemma was that any artist has to be an individual and any activist has to be part of a group. In everyday life that meant he had to be both at the same time, which was difficult enough.

It compounded the difficulty that Donnelly was not just another poet-politician. He insisted that his poetry was meaningless if separated from activism, and that his politics were useless unless based on individual insight. The forces that shaped his life and ideas were dialectically inter-related. The resolution of the contradictions that sprang from these forces gave strength to his politics and meaning to his poetry. Ultimately, his poems are as committed as his actions, and his actions as eloquent as his poems.

His last letters reveal the same pragmatic assessment of the dangers of his situation. He laughingly mentions the fact that he has not written enough for a full volume of his work, and that the world will never hear about so important a person. He took the danger of the war very seriously indeed, and yet his friends recall that he was elated during his last days in London. Having made his decision, he was determined to take part in the conflict that had been preoccupying his mind for six long months.

The Irish contingent had left Dublin, Belfast and Rosslare on 14 December,1936, travelling through London and France to Spain. From this we may assume that Donnelly was given a message on the fifteenth or sixteenth by one of the Irish contingent, with instructions to travel and details of where to join up with the Irish in Spain – the village of Madrigueras, near Albacete. He wrote a few goodbye notes, paid visits to various friends in London, and on 23 December, 1936 Charles Donnelly left Victoria

Station, travelling on a weekend ticket to Paris so that he could avoid using a passport.

He made his way south by train, probably to the French-Catalan coastal town of Perpignan, through which the Irish contingent had passed a few days earlier. From there he travelled to the Spanish border, crossing in secret around New Year's Eve. He continued to travel, down the Mediterranean coast. He arrived at Madrigueras and joined the Irish group on 7 January, 1937.

There was already terrible news. Eleven of the Irish fighters had been killed in the first few weeks, including a good friend of Donnelly's, Tommy Patton, a Communist from Achill Island. There were other problems also. The Irish section had been in training with the British group since their arrival at Madrigueras. But while Frank Ryan was away with the twelfth Italian and German Brigade in Madrid, tensions began to develop between the two units. The cause of this tension is still not fully clear. Ryan attributed it to the "stupidity and arrogance" of the British officers, whom he described, memorably, as "the swelled head adventurer type".

Brigade member Peter O'Connor from Waterford remembers the argument differently. He maintains that a number of the Irish group were unhappy about being with British soldiers, no matter what the officers were like. These were former IRA men who had devoted the best years of their lives to attacking British soldiers. They did not want to join up with them now. They wanted instead to join the American Abraham Lincoln Battalion, this unit contained many Irish-Americans. O'Connor's diary records that on 12 January, "a meeting which should never have taken place" was called to discuss the problem.

At that meeting, Charlie Donnelly, Johnny Power

and myself fought very hard to be sent to the British battalion. The main reason given by those who were for going to the Americans was because of the wrongs done to the Irish nation by the English in the past. They claimed that, though they were anti-fascist, they still looked on the English as the enemy. Those of us – and here I mention Charlie Donnelly in particular – pleaded passionately for a distinction to be made between anti-fascist working class comrades from England, and British Imperialism.

It was an understandable historical but political mistake that the vote went against us by such a small majority – five votes.[57]

The Irish section formed The James Connolly Column and moved to the village of Villanueva de la Jara to train with the Americans. According to O'Connor's diary, they arrived on 20 January, 1937, but Paul Burns, a member of the Lincoln Battalion, insists that it was earlier. In any case, the arrival of the fighting Irish was greeted with jubilation by the many Irish-American members of the battalion. Several of them, including Burns and the O'Flaherty brothers, Ed, Charlie and Frank, actually joined the Connolly Column, and they became good friends with Charles Donnelly.

Donnelly's training under the command of Captain Michael Kelly was basic but extremely strenuous. The climate was unpredictable, varying between great extremes of heat and cold. Conditions were bad and supplies were scarce. But the Irish soldiers, many of whom were hardened veterans of guerrilla warfare, were among the most eager to get into the fray. They trained enthusiastically by day, and at night they gathered in groups to drink, play cards and talk. A close group of comrades emerged, including Tommy Cox, Peter O'Connor, Paul Burns, the Flaherty brothers from Boston, and Charlie D, as Donnelly was nicknamed. They drank together, and visited the homes of the village of Villanueva. Their conversations covered all aspects of the war, and the various versions of it that appeared in the pro-Franco newspapers. The Americans were extremely interested in Irish politics, and Donnelly's spontaneous lectures on the Republican Congress, delivered in Spanish cantinas or olive groves, were effective in explaining its intricacies.

The men also talked about books and writers. Several of them had published poems and articles themselves, and they liked to discuss writers' attitudes towards the struggle against Fascism. However, shy to the last, Donnelly never told his friends about his own poetry. From time to time he would leave the company early, explaining that he had to write a few letters before lights out. Only after his death did his comrades discover that after slogging through the red mud of the training field all day, Donnelly was using his few spare hours to write poetry.

Only one poem survives which was written in Spain. This is the surrealistic and eerie "Heroic Heart".

> ... *Battering the roads, armoured columns*
> *Break walls of stone or bone without receipt.*
> *Jawbones find new ways with meat, loins*
> *Raking and blind, new ways with women.*

The poem suggests that pure rationality actually contains within itself the seeds of insanity and chaos. It is a powerful, prophetic and visionary piece of work, reminiscent in several senses of Yeats's "The Second Coming", a warning to ideologues and intellectuals about the importance of context in human affairs. It is a glimpse of what happens when thought is separated from action. Thought and action once again. The two poles of Charles Donnelly's life.

Donnelly seems genuinely to have liked Spain and the Spanish people. His letters are full of vivid descriptions of the countryside, the spirit of the peasant people and the high morale of his fellow fighters. In the very last letter, he sends his love to his family, through his brother, Tom, and he wishes for his family to be happy and unified once again.

But this wish was never to be realised. On the very day that his last letter was written, the battle began that was to claim Donnelly's life.

On 6 February,1937, Franco's army advanced into the Jarama valley in an attempt to capture the road between Madrid and Valencia. The British battalion was the first to be sent into action, but it became immediately clear that the Republican leaders had seriously underestimated the strength of the insurgent force. An urgent call was sent out for reinforcements. On 15 February the Lincoln Battallion received orders to cut short its training and move immediately to the front. The more experienced men in the Irish group had already gone into battle at Jarama. Frank Ryan had been wounded. Some of the men had been killed, among them Kit Conway, one of the first Irishmen to arrive in Spain, and one of the most courageous. The survivors fought on bravely, despite confused leadership and overwhelming opposition.

Meanwhile the Lincolns had left their base, with a strength of 450 men, divided into two infantry companies, a machine-gun unit and a group of paramedics and doctors. Donnelly and his comrades moved by truck to the brigade base at Albacete, where each man was given a rifle, a bayonet, an ammunition belt with 150 rounds. Up until this point the volunteers' training had been purely tactical. Guns and ammunition were too scarce to be wasted on teaching men how to use them. Consequently, this was the first time that Charles Donnelly had ever held a weapon in his hands. Many of his comrades were similarly inexperienced.

They left Albacete for the town of Morata de Tajuna, travelling slowly, under cover of darkness whenever this was possible. At some point in this hazardous journey the convoy of trucks was stopped, and the volunteers told to dismount and clean their rifles, which were still covered in the coating of protective grease in which they had been packed. No cleaning materials had been issued, so the men used their clothing, or bandages, whatever came to hand. The brigade members were then ordered to form into lines on each side of the road. Each man took it in turn to fire a few shots into the rocky hills. This done, they climbed back into the trucks and moved on to the front. Charles Donnelly's weapons training was over.

The men of the Lincoln Battalion arrived at the Jarama valley on 23 February to find the battle raging. The fascist and republican armies were dug into trenches at opposite ends of the valley, each side preparing for a drawn out and bloody conflict that was ultimately to last for a month. The terrain was rough and sparse, dotted with twisted olive trees and vines. Conditions were appalling. The trenches were filthy. Food and even basic medical supplies were scarce. The fight against Fascism must have suddenly seemed a long way from the street corners of Dublin and the rowdy cafes of London.

Morale, however, was still high. Donnelly was in cheerful mood, eager to participate in his first combat. The Lincoln attack began that afternoon, commanded by Captain Robert Merriman. As the first section of the first infantry company, the men of the James

Connolly Column spearheaded the attack. Donnelly fought bravely, and was at all times in the forefront of the action.

But the attack was badly planned. To this day, no one is fully sure who was in command of the republican forces at Jarama as the Lincolns began to advance and fight. The plan, such as it was, involved the Irish soldiers advancing deeply to probe the enemy line. But the advance went too far. The Connolly Column, along with the Cuban and American sections were all cut off. Paul Burns was to recall the events of this terrible day:

In one of those interludes beneath an olive tree I looked around. On my left was Charlie Donnelly. Beyond him the Cuban section stretched between the road on the extreme left and the Irish section. To the right of the Irish section, the American section dug in and fired.

A few yards away in a little hollow of earth was Captain John Scott, and with him Frank O'Flaherty, one of the three O'Flaherty brothers of Boston, who distinguished themselves by their heroic service and leadership under fire.

Donnelly joined me under an olive tree and we fired until our rifles burned our hands, with scarcely a word beyond the "Hi Charlie, how's it going?" and the reply, "Pretty good, how's the rest of the boys?"

The infantry continued the advance. Explosive bullets split the air and the machine-gun bursts raked the field. From behind a row of trees the fascists increased their fire. Captain Scott, rising, had only time to shout "Continue the advance", when he fell with three bullets in his body.[58]

Shortly after this incident Burns himself was wounded by machine-gun fire and taken to hospital.

He was never to see Charles Donnelly again. Bill Henry took over Scott's command. The battle went on and Henry was killed the next day. Eddie O'Flaherty became commander of the unit, which by now had dug in to regroup. Sporadic fighting and sniper fire continued. And then, on the evening of 27 February, a massive fascist advance began.

The men of the Canadian MacKenzie-Papineau Battalion were dug in beside the Lincolns. A member of the battalion wrote later:

We ran for cover. Charlie Donnelly, Commander of the Irish company is crouched behind an olive tree. He has picked up a bunch of olives from the ground and is squeezing them. I hear him say something quietly between a lull in machine-gun fire; "Even the olives are bleeding."[59]

A few minutes later, as Charles Donnelly was covering the retreat, he was caught in a burst of gunfire. He was struck three times, in the right arm, the right side, and the head. He collapsed and died instantly. There was no time to retrieve his body.

Charles Donnelly lay dead on the Spanish battlefield for ten days, while the bloody battle of Jarama raged on. On 9 March, following the fascist retreat, his body was found by Peter O'Connor.

O'Connor, with Peter and Johnny Power carried the body to a quiet olive grove. There was a short ceremony, and on 10 March 1937 Charles Patrick Donnelly was buried alongside several comrades, in an unmarked grave, in the valley of Jarama, in Spain.

He had told his comrades that he was twenty-six. He was actually twenty-two years of age.

POSTSCRIPT

Charles Donnelly had falsified his age when he joined the International Brigade, so news of his death did not reach Dublin for some time. His friends and his family were horrified. Blanaid Salkeld, Ewart Milne and Cecil Salkeld all wrote poems in tribute to him. So did his college friend, Donagh MacDonagh:

> *Of what a quality is courage made*
> *That he who gently walked our city streets*
> *Talking of poetry or philosophy,*
> *Spinoza, Keats,*
> *Should lie like any martyred soldier*
> *His brave and fertile brain dried quite away*
> *And the limbs that carried him from cradle to*
> *death's outpost*
> *Growing down into a foreign clay.*

Charles Donnelly's father was so distressed that he did not speak about his eldest son for many years. Cora Hughes and George Gilmore were absolutely shocked.

Cora died four years later, of tuberculosis. Gilmore was with her when she died, and he told me that her last thoughts were of Charlie Donnelly, the tender and courageous young poet with whom she had once fallen in love.

Having survived the 1916 Rising, the War of Independence, the Civil War, years of imprisonment and an airplane crash while on a mission to Spain in 1932, George Gilmore died in Dublin, in July 1985. A few months before his death, he told me that Charles Donnelly was the bravest man he had ever met.

During the battle of Jarama, twenty five thousand

of the Spanish Republican forces and many thousands of International Brigade members died, including nineteen Irishmen of the James Connolly Column. The battle lasted for over a month. There followed a seventy three day period of trench duty to defend the captured road.

On 21 September 1938, the Republican government announced that it was sending the International Brigade fighters home. Doctor Juan Negrín, the Prime Minister, explained regretfully that this was being done "to eliminate all pretexts and possible doubts about the genuinely national character of the cause for which the Republican army is fighting."[60] It was actually done in an attempt to force the withdrawal of the enormous Nazi-Italian-Portuguese battalions that had been fighting for Franco.

It did not work. In the coming months, more and more Fascist units from Germany and Italy arrived. The brave days of the Spanish Republic were numbered. Barcelona fell on 26 January, 1939.

On 28 March, 1939, Franco's army took Madrid. Two days later the Fascist victory was complete. There followed forty years of dictatorship in Spain.

Frank Ryan was arrested by an Italian unit on 31 March, 1938, and condemned to death by a court martial. This sentence was later commuted, and he was imprisoned at Burgos Prison until 14 July, 1940. He never recovered from the bad effect of prison life on his health, and he died in Berlin, on 10 June, 1944. Thirty five years later his body was brought back to Ireland. He was buried in Glasnevin cemetery on 22 June, 1979.

Fifty nine members of the James Connolly Column died fighting for the Spanish Republic. Most of the eighty five who survived left Spain on 6 December, 1938, with the farewell words of the great orator, Dolores Ibarruri – La Passionaria – ringing in their ears:

You came to us from all peoples, from all races. You came like brothers of ours, like sons of undying Spain. We shall not forget you, and when the olive tree of peace puts forth its leaves again, entwined with the laurels of the Spanish Republic's victory, – come back.

Come back to us. With us, those of you who have no country will find one. Those of you who have to live deprived of friendship will find friends. All of you will find the love and gratitude of the whole Spanish people who, now, and in the future, will cry out with all their hearts:

Long live the heroes of the International Brigades.[61]

For over thirty years Charles Donnelly was almost completely forgotten, except for a few brief references in histories of the Irish Left, or of the Spanish War. When his father died in 1969, Joe Donnelly began to recover the poems, political writings and essays of his elusive brother. Since then, very little of Charles Donnelly's work has been made available. Over a decade ago a pirated version of the poems appeared, allegedly published in Spain, but actually secretly printed in Dublin. In 1987, Joe Donnelly finally published a full edition of the poems, along with an account of his brother's life, which quickly went out of print.

Whatever I have quoted here is work now out of copyright. The rest of Charles Donnelly's work – his political journalism, his youthful short stories, his literary criticism, sections of his letters, his economic research, his military strategical and historical writings, his pamphlets, his articles on Fascism and the Spanish War, his extensive notes for a critical biography of James Connolly, and his explorations of the Marxist philosophy that shaped his life, – all these have remained largely unpublished, so far.

For these, we must wait a little longer.

A SELECTION OF
CHARLES DONNELLY'S
POEMS

DA MIHI

I

Give me thy speed, wild wailing Wind,
Thy never-ending speed be me!
That I may fly
Into the embrace of the sky,
Into the bosom of wild eyed eternity,
Eternity, whose darkness is an eye!
That I may cleave,
May, wild-souled, cleave
The shoreless waters of unending night,
That I may be
What human ne'er has been,
Wild spirit, bodiless and free,
Wild singing spirit of breast-bursting might!

II

Give me thy hotness, molten Sun,
Thy melting hotness be my soul!
That I may burn
An unquenched light;
That I may conquer
Deep-shouldered night;
That a star, shining bright,
I may be
Above the tumbling mountains of a night-cloaked
    sea,
Above the soul-strewn waters of eternity!
That my song-laden bark
May conquer the Dark,
That, girded in splendour, I may reach the goal!

III

Give me thy redness, love-sighing Rose,
Thy blushing tenderness be my heart!
That I may feel,
May, love-taught, feel
My fellow-creatures' woe;
That my song may be kind,
My verse warm, lined
With truth such as angels know;
That my youth-written book
Be a crystal brook
For the parched soul to drink deep!
As sweet as soft-shouldered nymphs' backward
    look,
From the fading island of rose-embowered sleep!

THE DEATH SONG

Burst from my breast, O my song, sweet song,
Like a gold tongued blast, O my song, sweet song,
Burst from me, and let me die!

For hate must die, and fear must die
And sorrow is not in the sky,
But tho' God crack Eternity
Love lives on!

This life is but a walking sleep
Above a dark unwanted Deep,
Then, waken soul, and wildly leap,
And Life is won!

Burst forth my song, to Eternity,
And thunder like the cave lunged sea,
And I, my song, will follow thee,
Will follow thee!

Will follow thee, will follow thee!
My song, thro' all Eternity,
My love-made soul will pale Death flee,
And follow thee!

And if love cannot live in life,
Then Death embrace, and leave the strife,
And take Eternity to wife,
And live in Death!

All live in Death, whose life was Love,
Whose Love was pure as the Vast Above,
Whose heart was eagle, whose heart was dove,
I'll live in Death!

I'll live in Death, a spirit free
A cool voiced mountain wind I'll be,
And thou, my love, will come with me,
To love in Death!

To love in Death, to love for ever,
In Death, warm love grows cooler never,
And Death's pale eyes can never sever
Who love in Death!
Who live in Death!

TO YOU

In the old days of bitter faces
And cold eyes,
I would go to the lone, large places, the hills
And the skies,
To the twilight of grey, great shadows
And bird cries ...
And shadows would hide me, and the wind sighed
With my sighs ...
But you, my Jewess, having come, and gone,
Whence can I bring my soul,
When the winds but mock, and the shadows
Bring mirrors of thy soul?

AT THE DREAMING OF THE DREAMS

My dreams are dreaming, and the sacred books
Have closed their lips, and smothered up their lies,
And all the worlds are whirling in the skies,
And all the skies are like a woman's looks.

I live, I live, and yet I reck it not.
I am one with the depths and with the heights,
I am beyond the fadings of the lights
Of all the suns. I live, and yet live not.

The murmur of the waters of all
Being is me; the silence of undying Death.
Eternity breathes in me, and its breath
Is Death in hand with Life, Unbeing with Being.

The bosom of God's parent, boundless Sleep,
Enfolds me, and I drown within the eyes,
The smiling eyes that are a woman's eyes,
The eyes of all the soul of all the Deep.

And all the dreamings of the dreams of God
Are burning from me, like a woman's love,
I fade and melt in Space, below, above,
And God is in my being, I in God.

Oh, all men's toil to prove true the great lie
Of the world, like staring in a sea
To find the secret of its blue, while He
Above reflects it from the waters of His eye.

Oh, all the world is but an endless lie,
Eternity and Space a swirling dream.
My soul is like the murmur of a stream.
I dream within a dream. To live, to die,
To be, or not to be, matters not, dream I.

THE DEAD
With apologies to – Myself

What ghastly sight is this, within the Hall
A row of tombstones lined along the wall.
Ah, here they lie, the Muse's valiant slain,
Of that brave band, does not one soul remain?
There does. See lone O'Phelan, mourning in the Main.
E'en as I look, he raises his lorn head,
And thus makes sad lament above the Dead:
"Of late a faction rose with much uproar,
Turning their heads – which had been turned before –
But, ah, their little day was quickly o'er ... –"
("Praised be the Lord!" say I, between my sighs).
But deaf in grief, O'Phelan said: "Here lies
Caomhighin, who held, the dignity of our sex
In stride abides not, but in hornrimmed specs,
For with their aid – I libel the anoint –
He could see everything (except the point)!
Cox, who lies here, at rhetoric adept,
Raged at his audience, while his audience slept;
While he waxed wroth about Freemasonry
The ladies amorous waxéd ('bout buns and tea).
Here Barnabas was thrown, whose Muse being lame,
He mistook notoriety for fame;
Loved of the ladies, as orator had he
Every gift – save that of orat'ry;
But, ah, although we smiled whene'er he "spoke"
We smiled not when he joked – that was no joke!
Our JFK lies here, whose pen, my lad,
Had tons of dignity ('twas all it had);
Champion he was, and champion resplendent,
Of faith, and morals, and the "Independent".

Now he lies here, along with many more,
Who were a merry company of yore
And raised dust and the devil in Sixth-Four........"
I left him there, my eyes with tears being blind,
To write about it to "The Catholic Mind".

IN A LIBRARY

Are the moods voiceless? For I have no words.
Blood cannot talk, although it crack the skin.
Red hots and colds are pumped up from the pit
Like hungering men; and no word-woman being
    near, sink again howling in.
And I fume, and look outside on the grey
Wind hammered to fantasy day.

STASIS

I
The silent light descends
Like a cloth over me
Here under the trees
Whose presence has infolded on itself
And the monotone
Of the afar-falling waters pours over my mind.
The rising thoughts level before it
And as seeds borne by the wind
Are borne away from me.
Thoughts go. Thoughts bend, break, float away.

II
This is a sleeping place,
A cast shell
Of the snail of the world,
A thing left in a crevice.

SMALL BIRDS SEEN THROUGH TENUOUS TREES

Small birds seen through tenuous trees
spin out in flickering Time a
past scent of hay, dew on the cold gate-lock.
On the reach of a tactile prong
is superimposed a line of Keats.
The soul of Mr Powell purrs
among the kerbstones' interstices
which raise it toward an image-synthesis.
Between the quality of female fingers
and its ramifications
his soul appraises its delicate oscillations.

O in the globed air of a thought-fusion
how satisfying
a sun-spurted series of ledges,
a match box,
a foot
springing.
Through streets and the well-considered trees
("No too elaborate tapestries
let just the gesture, the emphasis"),
Mr Powell's subtle soul
propels finely.
"The thin fine thread of my desire"
vaguely consummated on a garden wall
(Three blades of grass and red dust).
"How thrilling, and, indeed,
a quite valid emotion".

APPROACH

The tightening eyes, tendrilled of sympathy,
The accepted secret before a third;
The unrequired gesture, imperfect denial of contact,

The flaunt, the posture, display of the self,
Under appraisal relenting to seriousness,
And sudden tenderness lightening in sudden actions;

The gaze, responded to, steadying in brave request;
Prolonged at acceptance, the attitude
Breaking in mutual and offered laughter.

STORY: WRITTEN IN DEPRESSION AT A DEBATE
ON THE ESSENCE OF POETRY.

Bang
down the riverside
extenuating circumstances while temporary insane
why did his wife?

Angry words to false emotions often lead astray
I have been led away.
Requiescat.

THE FLOWERING BARS

After sharp words from the fine mind,
protest in court,
the intimate high head constrained,
strait lines of prison, empty walls,
a subtle beauty in a simple place.

There to strain thought through the tightened brain,
there weave the slender cords of thought, in calm,
until routine in prospect bound
joy into security,
and among strictness sweetness grew,
mystery of flowering bars.

THE TOLERANCE OF CROWS

Death comes in quantity from solved
Problems on maps, well-ordered dispositions,
Angles of elevation and direction;

Comes innocent from tools children might
Love, retaining under pillows,
Innocently impales on any flesh.

And with flesh falls apart the mind
That trails thought from the mind that cuts
Thought clearly for a waiting purpose.

Progress of poison in the nerves and
Discipline's collapse is halted.
Body awaits the tolerance of crows.

POEM

Between rebellion as a private study and the public
Defiance, is simple action only on which will flickers
Catlike, for spring. Whether at nerve roots is secret
Iron, there's no diviner can tell, only the moment can
  show.
Simple and unclear moment, on a morning utterly
  different
And under circumstances different from what you'd
  expected.

Your flag is public over granite. Gulls fly above it.
Whatever the issue of the battle is, your memory
Is public, for them to pull awry with crooked hands,
Moist eyes. And village reputations will be built on
Inaccurate accounts of your campaign. You're name
  for orators,
Figure stone-struck beneath damp Dublin sky.

In a delaying action, perhaps, on hillside in remote
  parish,
Outposts correctly placed, retreat secured to wood,
  bridge mined
Against pursuit, sniper may sight you carelessly
  contoured.
Or death may follow years in strait confinement,
  where diet
Is uniform as ceremony, lacking only fruit.
Or on the barrack square before the sun casts
  shadow.

Name, subject of all-considered words, praise and
    blame,
Irrelevant, the public talk which sounds the same on
    hollow
Tongue as true, you'll be with Parnell and with
    Pearse.
Name aldermen will raise a cheer with, teachers
    make reference
Oblique in class, and boys and women spin gum of
    sentiment
On qualities attributed in error.

Man, dweller in mountain huts, possessor of
    coloured mice,
Skilful in minor manual turns, patron of obscure
    subjects, of
Gaelic swordsmanship and mediaeval armoury.
The technique of the public man, the masked
    servilities are
Not for you. Master of military trade, you give
Like Raleigh, Lawrence, Childers, your services but
    not yourself.

HEROIC HEART

Ice of heroic heart seals plasmic soil
Where things ludicrously take root
To show in leaf kindness time had buried
And cry music under a storm of 'planes,
Making thrust head to slacken, muscle waver
And intent mouth recall old tender tricks.
Ice of heroic heart seals steel-bound brain.

There newer organs built for friendship's grappling
Waste down like wax. There only leafless plants
And earth retain disinterestedness.
Thought, magnetised to lie of the land, moves
Heartily over the map wrapped in its iron
Storm. Battering the roads, armoured columns
Break walls of stone or bone without receipt.
Jawbones find new ways with meat, loins
Raking and blind, new ways with women.

NOTES

1 Cardinal Logue and Archbishops and Bishops of Ireland, Pastoral Letter, (22 October 1922).

2 Joseph Donnelly, interview with the author, 10 March, 1986.

3 Charles Donnelly, "The Case of the Rifled Safe" in *Our Boys*, (Dublin, 13 November 1933).

4 Cardinal MacRory and Archbishops and Bishops of Ireland, Pastoral Letter, (18 October 1931).

5 Niall Sheridan, interview in BBC Radio Northern Ireland documentary, "Even The Olives are Bleeding", date unavailable.

6 ibid.

7 Charles Donnelly, "Philistia", in *Cothrom Féinne*, (UCD, 17 March 1932) p.179

8 Charles Donnelly, "The Death Song", in *Cothrom Féinne*, (UCD, December 1931) p.122.

9 Charles Donnelly, "People", in *Cothrom Feinne*, (UCD, April (1932) p. 235.

10 Charles Donnelly, "Gifford Redidivus", in *Cothrom Féinne*, (UCD, March 1932) p.159.

11 ibid.

12 Charles Donnelly, "Literature in Ireland", in *Cothrom Féinne*, (UCD, May 1933) p.65.

13 Charles Donnelly, "The Trend of Modern Philosophy", in *Cothrom Féinne*, (UCD, April 1934) p.18.

14 ibid.

15 Donagh MacDonagh, "Charlie Donnelly", in *The Irish Times*, (Dublin, 15 March 1941) p. 11.

16 ibid.

17 Charles Donnelly, op. cit., 12.

18 Niall Sheridan, op. cit. 5.

19 Charles Donnelly, "Alas Poor Hamlet", in *Cothrom Féinne*,

(UCD, November 1933) p.25.

20 Donagh MacDonagh, op. cit., 15.

21 Niall Sheridan, op. cit. 5.

22 ibid.

23 Allen Tate, 1937, quoted in Francis Hope, "The Thirties", in Ian Hamilton (ed.), *The Modern Poet: Essays From "The Review"*, (London, 1968) p. 83.

24 Michael Roberts, *Critique of Poetry*, (London, 1934) p. 238.

25 Charles Donnelly, op. cit., 12.

26 WH Auden, "Authority in America", in *The Griffin*, (London, 1935) p.21.

27 George Gilmore, *Republican Congress*, (Dublin, 1969) p.47.

28 Barbara Redmond, interview in BBC Radio Northern Ireland documentary, "Even the Olives are Bleeding", date unavailable.

29 George Gilmore, interview with the author, January 1985.

30 Quoted in *An Phoblacht*, (Dublin, 24 October 1931) p.7.

31 Robin Skelton, *Poetry of the Thirties*, (Harmondsworth, 1964) p.36.

32 Samuel Hynes, *The Auden Generation: Literature and Politics in the 1930's*, (London, 1976) p.135.

33 Pablo Neruda, "Explico Algunas Cosas" ("I Am Explaining a Few Things"), in *Selected Poems*, ed. Nathaniel Tarn, (London, 1970) p.103.

34 GS Fraser, "Elusive Honesty: The Poetry of Louis McNiece", in his *Vision and Rhetoric: Studies in Modern Poetry*, (London, 1959) p.179.

35 Michael O'Riordan, *Connolly Column*, (Dublin, 1979) p. 76.

36 George Gilmore, op. cit., 27, p.54.

37 ibid., p.64.

38 George Gilmore, interview with the author, January 1985.

39 Charles Donnelly, "Can We Get Unity On This Basis", in *Republican Congress*, (28 September 1935) p.3.

40 ibid.

41 George Gilmore, interview with the author, January 1985.

42 Charles Donnelly, "Reform, Insurrection and Revolution", in *Republican Congress*, (5 October 1935) p.2.

43 ibid.

44 ibid.

45 Charles Donnelly, "Democracy, Fascism and Class", in
   Cothrom Féinne, (UCD, April 1934) p.11.

46 Charles Donnelly, "Al Capone Was One of the Fascist Patriots",
   in *Republican Congress*, (3 November 1934) p.2.

47 Quoted in Charles Donnelly, "The Irish Republic at the
   Crossroads", unpublished manuscript in the possession of the
   Donnelly family.

48 Charles Donnelly and "Ajax", (Montague Slater), "Connolly and
   Casement", in *Left Review*, (London, April 1936) p.290.
   "Wallace" is probably William Wallace, Scottish patriot hanged
   in London in 1305.

49 Speech by H McMorrow, reported in *The Irish Independent*,
   (Dublin, 1 September 1936), p.7.

50 *The Irish Independent*, (Dublin, 8 September 1936) p.12.

51 Aodh de Blacam, *For God and Spain*, (Dublin, 1936). De
   Blacam wrote for the *Irish Press* under the pen-name "Roddy
   the Rover."

52 Niall Sheridan, op.cit. 5.

53 Frank Ryan, quoted in Sean Cronin, *Frank Ryan: The Search
   for the Republic*.

54 George Gilmore, interview with the author, January 1985.

55 Hugh MacDiarmaid, *Speaking for Scotland*, (Baltimore, 1946)
   p.29.

56 John Cornford, "Full Moon at Tiers", quoted in Hugh Ford, *A
   Poet's War: British Poets in the Spanish Civil War*, (London
   and Philadelphia, 1965) p.120

57 Peter O'Connor, letter to the editor, *Irish Democrat*, (London,
   December 1978).

58 See Edwin Rolfe, *The Lincoln Battalion*, (New York, 1939)
   p.67.

59 ibid., p.75.

60 Quoted in O'Riordan, *Connolly Column*, (Dublin, 1971) p. op.
   cit., p130.

61 From text of speech by La Passionaria, 29 October 1938. A
   copy was given to each member of the International Brigades.
   Quoted in O'Riordan, *Connolly Column*, (Dublin, 1979) p. 135

A CHARLES DONNELLY BIBLIOGRAPHY

SECTION A: WORK BY CHARLES DONNELLY

(1) THE SURVIVING POEMS:

"On First Hearing John Count McCormack", (1929). Manuscript in the possession of the Donnelly family.

"Da Mihi", in *Cothrom Féinne*, (University College Dublin, November 1931) p.87.

"The Death Song", in *Cothrom Féinne*, (University College Dublin, December 1931) p. 123.

"To You", in *Cothrom Féinne*, (University College Dublin, March 1932) p.205.

"At the Dreaming of the Dreams", in *The National Student*, (Dublin, May 1932) p.47.

"To a Bad Critic", in *Cothrom Féinne*, (University College Dublin, June 1932) p.243.

"The Dead", in *Cothrom Féinne*, (University College Dublin, November 1932) p.75.

"In a Library", in *Motley* magazine, (The Gate Theatre, Dublin, January 1933) p.10.

"The Professor", (May, 1933). Manuscript in the possession of the Donnelly family.

"Stasis", in *Cothrom Féinne*, (University College Dublin, November 1933) p.37.

"Small Birds Seen Through Tenuous Trees", in *Cothrom Féinne*, (University College Dublin, March 1934) p.69.

"Approach", in *Cothrom Féinne*, (University College Dublin, April 1934) p.4.

"Mister Sheridan's Morning Prayer", in *Cothrom Féinne*, (University College Dublin, May 1934) p.32.

"Story: Written in Depression at a Debate on the Essence of Poetry", in *Cothrom Féinne*, (University College Dublin, May 1934) p.38.

"Wages of Deviation", (1934). Manuscript in the possession of the Donnelly family.

"Unnoticed in Hurry of Callous Goodbye", (1934). Manuscript in the possession of the Donnelly family.

"Music, Nice Turns of Thought", with Cecil Ffrench Salkeld, (1935). Manuscript in the possession of the Donnelly family.

"The Flowering Bars", in Leslie Daiken, (ed.), *Goodbye Twilight*, (London, 1936) p.30.

"Poem", in *Ireland Today*, (Dublin, January 1937).

"The Tolerance of Crows", in *Ireland Today*, (Dublin, February 1937).

"Heroic Heart", in *Ireland Today*, (Dublin, July 1937)

In addition to these finished works there are three short fragments numbered 1, 2 and 3, deciphered and reproduced in MA thesis *The Life and Work of Charles Donnelly* by the present author, (University College Dublin, 1986).

(2) CHARLES DONNELLY: PUBLISHED SHORT FICTION

"The Case of the Rifled Safe", in *Our Boys*, (Dublin, November 1930).

"The Amateur Criminal", in *Our Boys*, (Dublin, March 1931).

"The Gunman", by Francis Nolan, pseudonym for Charles Donnelly, in *Our Boys*, (Dublin, May 1931).

"The Death Song", in *Cothrom Féinne*, (University College Dublin, December 1931).

"Philistia: an Allegory", in *Cothrom Féinne*, (University College Dublin, March 1932).

"People", in *Cothrom Féinne*, (University College Dublin, April 1932).

(3) CHARLES DONNELLY: UNPUBLISHED SHORT FICTION

Untitled story about "Maureen", (c.1929). Manuscript in the possession of the Donnelly family. Deciphered and quoted in MA thesis on Donnelly by the present author (UCD, 1986).

Untitled story about "Mister Walshe," the carpenter to whom Donnelly was apprenticed briefly, (c. 1929/1930). Manuscript in the possession of the Donnelly family. Deciphered and quoted in MA thesis on Donnelly by the present author (UCD, 1986).

Untitled short story about pickets, (c. 1934?). Manuscript in the possession of the Donnelly family.

"Life and Opinions", (c. 1935). Manuscript in the possession of the Donnelly family. Full copy in MA thesis on Donnelly by the present author, (UCD, 1986).

"A Nation Awake", (c.1935). Manuscript in the possession of the Donnelly family.

(4) CHARLES DONNELLY: PUBLISHED JOURNALISM AND CRITICAL WRITING

"Gifford Redidivus", in *Cothrom Féinne*, (UCD, March 1932).

"Letter to the Editor", in *Cothrom Féinne*, (UCD, April 1932).

"Literature in Ireland", in *Cothrom Féinne*, (UCD, May 1933).

"Alas Poor Hamlet", in *Cothrom Féinne*, (UCD, November 1933).

"Democracy, Fascism and Class", in *Cothrom Féinne*, (UCD, April 1934).

"The Trend of Modern Philosophy", in *Cothrom Féinne*, (UCD, April 1934).

"The Royal Breed", in *Republican Congress*, (Dublin, date unavailable, c. November 1934).

"De Valera in Griffith's Shoes", in *Republican Congress*, (Dublin, date unavailable, c. November 1934).

"Al Capone Was One Of The Fascist Patriots", in *Republican Congress*, (Dublin, 3 November 1934).

"A Plan for the Tenants' Housing Fight", in *Republican Congress*, (Dublin, 22 December 1934).

"Republicans and a National Plebiscite", in *Republican Congress*, (Dublin, 22 December 1934).

"Fianna Fail's Road to the Republic", in *Irish Front*, (London, March 1935).

"Get Into Harness: A Leaflet Draft", in *Irish Front*, (London, March 1935).

"The Popular Front and Imperial Policy", in *Irish Front*, (London, March 1935).

"An Open Letter to a London Irishman", in *Irish Front*, (London, April 1935).

"Turn the Economic War into a War for the Republic", in *Irish Front*, (London, May 1935).

"They Ask a Permit for Freedom Now", in *Republican Congress*, (Dublin, 18 May 1935).

"Ireland Fights For Freedom", in *The Daily Worker*, (London, 25 May 1935).

"When Rogues Fall Out", in *Irish Front*, (London, June 1935).

"England and Italy Are Lining Up For War", in *Republican Congress*, (Dublin, 13 July 1935).

"Britain's Game of Choose the Loser", in *Republican Congress*, (Dublin, 10 August 1935).

"Can We Get Unity On This Basis?", in *Republican Congress*, (Dublin, 28 September 1935).

"Reform, Insurrection and Revolution", in *Republican Congress*, (Dublin, 5 October 1935).

"Portrait of a Revolution", in *Left Review*, (London, October 1935).

"Ireland's Duty to Peace", in *Irish Front*, (London, October 1935).

"What the Connolly Tradition Demands Today", in *Republican Congress*, (Dublin, 21 December 1935).

"Connolly and Casement", in *Left Review*, (London, April 1936).

"The Edinburgh Conference and the Empire", in *Irish Front*, (London, October 1936).

"The Irish Christian Front", in *Irish Front*, (London, October 1936).

(5) CHARLES DONNELLY: UNPUBLISHED JOURNALISM AND CRITICAL WRITING

The following manuscripts are in the possession of the Donnelly family:

"Fascism and the Humanist Outlook", (c.1935). Political essay.

"Europe and Fascism", (c.1935/36).

"Realism and the Contemporary Subject", (c.1935/36).

"The Irish Banking System", (c.1936). Research piece commissioned by British Labour Research Bureau.

"Labour and the Empire: A Conference Report", (c. 1936).

"The Popular Front and Imperial Policy", (c. 1936).

"The Strategy of Insurrection", (1936) Notes on military strategy.

"The Irish Republic at the Crossroads", (1936).

"The Spanish Civil War", (1936). Two sets of notes.

"Irregular Armies and Modern Technique", (1936).

"Notes for a Critical Biography of James Connolly", (1936). These scattered notes have been collected, reconstructed and edited together to form an essay in MA thesis on Donnelly by the present author (UCD, 1986).

(6) CHARLES DONNELLY: UNPUBLISHED LETTERS

These original manuscripts and copies of letters from Charles Donnelly are all in the possession of the Donnelly family:

To Donagh and Maura MacDonagh, 6 November 1936.

To Cecil Salkeld, 26 November 1936.

To Maura MacDonagh, 5 December 1936.

To Donagh and Maura MacDonagh, 16 December 1936.

To Donagh MacDonagh, 19 December 1936.

To Cecil Salkeld, 21 December 1936.

To Tom Donnelly, 2 December 1937.

To Tom Donnelly, 6 February 1937.

SECTION B: CRITICISM AND COMMENT ON CHARLES DONNELLY

(1) PUBLISHED ARTICLES ON CHARLES DONNELLY

Boland, Eavan, "In Search of a Poet", in *The Irish Times*, (Dublin, 2 June 1975).

Cronin, Sean, "An Irish Poet in Spain", in *The Irish Times*, (Dublin, 18 December 1970).

Donnelly,Joseph, *Charles Donnelly: The Life and Poems*,(Dedalus Press, Dublin, 1987)

Kemmy, Jim, "He is Dead and Gone, Lady", in *New Hibernia*, (Dublin, July 1986).

MacDonagh, Donagh, "Charlie Donnelly", in *The Irish Times*, (Dublin, 15 March, 1941).

Milne, Ewart, "A Memory of Charlie Donnelly", in *Iron* magazine, (place and date of publication unavailable).

O'Connor, Peter, Letter to the Editor, *Irish Democrat*, (London, December, 1978).

Slater, Montague, "Charles Donnelly", in *Left Review*, (London, July, 1937).

Smith, Michael, "Charles Donnelly", in *The Lace Curtain*, (Dublin, Summer 1971).

There is also a good brief critical section on Donnelly by Declan Kiberd, in Seamus Deane (ed.), *The Field Day Anthology of Irish Literature*, (Dublin, 1991).

(2) UNPUBLISHED ARTICLES ON CHARLES DONNELLY

The Donnelly family is in possession of a number of unpublished memoirs of Charles Donnelly. These are by Paul Burns, Paddy Byrne, Leslie Daiken, Montague Slater and Niall Sheridan.

Extracts from these are included in MA thesis on Donnelly by the present author.

SECTION C: GENERAL BACKGROUND WORKS

Alexander, Bill, *British Volunteers for Liberty: Spain 1936-1939*, (London, 1982).

Alvarez, A, *The Shaping Spirit*, (London, 1958).

Anon., *Romanceros de los Voluntarios de la Libertad*, (Madrid, 1937).

Auden, WH, *Collected Poetry*, (New York, 1954).

Auden, WH, "Introduction", in *Oxford Poetry*, (Oxford, 1927).

Auden, WH (ed.), *The Poet's Tongue: An Anthology*, (London, 1935).

Bergonzi, Bernard, *Reading the Thirties: Texts and Contexts*, (London, 1978).

Carter, Ronald (ed.), *Thirties Poets: The Auden Group*, (London, 1984).

Caudwell, Christopher, *Illusion and Reality*, (London, 1937).

Caudwell, Christopher, *Poems*, (London, 1939).

Cornford, John, *Understand the Weapon, Understand the Wound*, (Manchester, 1976).

Cronin, Sean, *Frank Ryan: The Search for the Republic*, (Dublin, 1980).

Cunningham, Valentine, (ed.), *Spanish Front: Writers on the Spanish Civil War*, (Oxford, 1986).

Day Lewis, Cecil, *A Hope for Poetry*, (Oxford, 1934).

Day Lewis, Cecil, "Revolutionaries and Poetry", in *Left Review*, (London, October 1936).

Fraser, GS, *Vision and Rhetoric: Studies in Modern Poetry*, (London, 1959).

Gilmore, George, *Republican Congress*, (Dublin, 1969).

Hope, Francis, "The Thirties", in Ian Hamilton (ed.), *The Modern Poet: Essays from "The Review"*, (London, 1968).

Hynes, Samuel, *The Auden Generation: Literature and Politics in England in the 1930's*, (London, 1976).

MacNiece, Louis, "A Statement", in *New Verse*, (London, Autumn 1938).

O'Donnell, Peadar, *"Salud": An Irishman in Spain*, (London, 1937).

O'Riordan, Michael, *Connolly Column*, (Dublin, 1979).

Rickword, Edgell, "Writers in Spain", in *Left Review*, (September, 1937).

Rolfe, Edmund, *The Lincoln Battalion*, (New York, 1939).

Skelton, Robin, (ed.), *Poetry of the Thirties*, (Harmondsworth, 1964).

Spender, Stephen, "A Conversation with Stephen Spender", in *The Review*, (London, 1970)

Spender, Stephen, "The Problems of Poet and Public", in *The Spectator*, (London, 3 August 1929).

Thomas, Hugh, *The Spanish Civil War*, (New York, 1961).

INDEX

141